Diary of a
WANNABE PHILOSOPHER

Book One

I0149306

Hilda de la Rosa

DEDICATION

To Richard.

My friend,

You left too soon.

ISBN 978-0-620-81778-3 (print) | ISBN 978-0-620-81779-0 (E-book)

LK Publishers books may be ordered on many online platforms or by contacting:
Lokinwi Publishers (Pty) Ltd Trading as: LK Publishers

www.LKPublishers.co.za

LK
PUBLISHERS
making a difference

ACKNOWLEDGMENTS

Without life's challenges, wisdom is not likely to be attained. Therefore, I want to acknowledge and thank life itself. The old Chinese curse, "May you have an interesting life," certainly applies to me. I have most certainly had an interesting and challenging life and just recently someone suggested that I write my life story but as a series of short stories. The friend suggested that if I put all the stories in one book, people may not believe that I experienced everything that I did.

This forms part of Diary of a Wannabe Philosopher - some of the insights that came about as a result of life's experiences. The knocks of life, the highs and the lows, the joys and the sorrows are what brings us to today. Without those experiences, we will not be who we are. We do, of course, have a choice. We can become victims of an *interesting life* or we can rise above the painful events in our past and allow those events to bring about resilience, courage, wisdom and ultimately, love. I thank every single person that brought an experience to my life – both the good experiences and the challenging ones. I certainly would not have the insight that I do without that.

There are a few people I wish to thank in particular. To my son, Clinton, who has provided me with much love, learning, insight, joy and consternation. Being a mom is really hard and is the closest thing we have to experiencing unconditional love. To my family who are always there, I know that I am not a *standard edition* and I know that it often confounds you. Thank you for your love.

Thank you to all the people who believe in me, who have influenced my life and who bring much love into my world. Kym, Herma, Friedel, Cameron, Roy, Tshidi, Sandra, Mom, Colleen, Walter, Sanette, Mel, Karen, Nieces and nephews and their spouses and delightful children, Dad, Lara, Miemsie, Luis, Priscilla, Megan, Pam, Farhana, JP, Mellissie, Craig, my brothers and their wives, Nicole, Diane, Ian, Vanessa, my sisters and their husbands, Carmel, Tersia, Richard, Lorna, Michael, Donald, Elisabeth, to name a few.

This book would not be in your hands if it were not for Latiefa, Gregg and Kathy, to whom I am forever grateful.

INTRODUCTION

My life irrevocably changed on the 29th August 2014. I was celebrating with my brother, his wife, and Roy, my beloved partner. My brother had just secured a lucrative contract and he and his wife had come to our home to celebrate their success. I was busy making dinner and I told Roy that I was about ready to serve it. Normally, he needed a ten-minute warning, so he had enough time to wash up before he joined us at the table. I did not hear any water running in the bathroom and after five minutes, I went to see what was delaying him. I found Roy in the bedroom, slumped over the bed. He was on his knees in front of the bed and his torso was resting on the bed with his hands tucked beneath him. It looked like he was in prayer. Instantly, I knew he was dead.

The love story between Roy and I is described in detail in my previous book entitled, *Love Versus Fear. Diary of a Wannabe Philosopher Book 1*, is partly a collection of my thoughts and feelings after the loss of Roy. I offer nothing other than murmurings. I hope that some of these murmurings will help others to deal with loss and perhaps it will provide some insights about life, love, and everything else.

Loss is a strange thing and we all deal with it in different ways. I have since learned that worrying about others while we are in the process of mourning is counter-productive. I have been a spiritual teacher for many years and, therefore, this book will be filled with my understanding of spirituality. It contains what I hope is some inspiration for you to feel understood, or to make you think and contemplate.

My understanding of life and spirituality is just that – my understanding. I have no requirement that you believe as I believe, and I have no intention of making any other belief system wrong. I have found what works for me. Perhaps, if I am lucky, some of it will work for you.

I feel quite strongly about maintaining my authentic personality and this book contains some profanity. I trust you have the emotional maturity to accept that it is not my intention to shock you. It is just who I am.

As I paged through my diary, I noticed a repetition of similar topics. I have left it like that. I feel that those topics are repeated probably because we need to hear them more than once. I believe that each time a topic is repeated, a slightly different view will be expressed. I know I need to hear some stuff fairly often just to remind me again of who I am and who I choose to be in this moment.

I do believe that each and every one of us has a choice, in every minute of every day. We can choose love, we can choose kindness, we can choose tolerance, and we can choose peace. Sometimes we don't. I don't beat myself up when I don't. I simply know that in every moment of every day, I can choose again. Falling into old, tired, negative behaviour patterns is part of life. Knowing that we can choose again, is liberating. I choose love.

CONTENTS

KARMA - IT IS SO MISUNDERSTOOD

11th May 2015

Karma is neither good nor bad. It just is. Most importantly, it is a *shared* experience. We have agreements with other souls to come to this planet to learn a specific lesson or lessons. We learn from our soul buddies, and together we have agreements to experience the positive and the negative aspect of an experience, or a thing, whatever that thing is.

Only when we have had this positive and negative experience of a thing several times, do we get to a space of acceptance or neutrality. Therefore, any experience is really a holy trinity, positive, negative and neutral. Neutrality equals mastery of a specific thing – and mastery is the goal - mastery of all things.

That doesn't mean that we lack compassion about that thing. In fact, quite the opposite. If we have *mastered* or reached neutrality about a thing, we should really have *more* compassion for those who have yet to reach neutrality about that thing. It is here where I think, "There but for the grace of God, go I."

Since humans are slow learners, we need to learn about one thing over and over again, before we *get* it. For example, we do not learn to *understand* the concept of blame and we won't learn how to *let go of* blame in one lifetime. It takes many lifetimes to

1

get past the blame game and for me, it's one of the most trying things to extricate myself from. It's easy to blame because it makes us feel better about who we are.

Let's look at a situation that we may be in from our own perspective, a situation where we feel fully entitled to blame another for our own unhappiness. Let's say we are married, and our partner has an affair. We are hurt and indignant about this cheater. We file for divorce and take the house and the car and make life impossible for our spouse. We even make it difficult for our ex-spouse to spend time with our children. We feel that if we withhold our children from our ex, they may begin to understand the pain they caused us and therefore, this may teach them a lesson. We may even say, "Karma will get him/her, just wait and see." Nope, it won't.

Now let's look at the fallout from a blame game perspective. We, from our perspective, tell all our friends that our spouse cheated on us after 25 years of marriage. We feel outraged and we want our friends to validate our feelings. We blather on about how hurt we are, and how sad the story really is. We proclaim to the world that karma will sort it out in the end. We hope that our ex will get what they deserve.

Our ex-spouse, on the other hand, tells his/her friends how neglected he/she felt and how we did not love or respect them. They talk about how lonely they were in our marriage, which can fully justify why they had an affair. People have affairs because they feel neglected and unloved. They will tell their friends that everyone deserves love and respect. They may point out how unfair it is that their ex is making it difficult for them to see their children. They tell their friends that their ex has taken everything from them: the house, the car, and now the children, who become a vengeance tool in the blame game. They also seek validation for their feelings from their friends.

In the meantime, our soul buddy, who is our ex-spouse in this lifetime, agreed, long before we incarnated in these bodies, that we would teach each other about the blame game in this lifetime. If we are truly becoming more evolved, we would have been able to get through this experience with love, understanding and compassion. Perhaps it was our soul agreement to find out if we really could overcome our differences and finally get to a point where both of us could take responsibility for *our* share in the drama.

This situation is what I call a karmic ribbon. A karmic ribbon is an intense emotional experience that links two people. Each of us experiences the karmic ribbon from *our* perspective. Both feel hurt and both feel wronged. Neither is right and neither is wrong. It is an experience called the blame game.

In this example, as in most, there is no absolute truth, there is always only our perspective of it. Karma is not a punishment, it is a reciprocal learning tool. All the experiences we have, we share with our soul buddies. Sometimes, our soul buddies are our mothers, they are our lovers, they are our business partners, they are our uncles, our friends, and our children.

According to Michael, my spiritual master-teacher, we surround ourselves with the same basic 300 souls and we experience different things together to achieve mastery - mastery about *everything*. Sometimes it is hard for us. I get that. I don't claim that it is easy.

When we have achieved mastery of all things, perhaps we will be evolved enough to go to a planet where there is not so much pain, a planet where we can truly experience peace, harmony, unconditional love, and total respect.

From what I observe, we are nowhere near achieving that. This is an experience called earth and it is not for sissies. Here we learn about opposites, such as darkness and light, hunger and abundance, joy and pain and, hopefully, when we have experienced these over many lifetimes, we can achieve mastery.

Karma is not a punishment for a perceived wrong of another. Let us be more aware of how we are simply changing the *words,* instead of changing our belief system. Replacing words such as heaven and hell, with ascension and karma is not growth or evolution. It is the same old, tired judgmental nonsense.

RESENTMENT

14th July 2015

Many people seem to be unhappy. It seems that there is an underlying mid-range murmur of resentment that fills most people's lives. Some can't really define why they are unhappy - they just are.

As we grow up and mature, we place all of our negative experiences in what I call a black box of resentment. These resentments can vary from something simple, from feeling that you are the only one who always makes the coffee, to feeling like the one who must take responsibility for everything.

Resentment is a funny thing, it kind of creeps up on one. We take on more than we should, and we take it on because we are not able to say no. Good girls and boys don't say no. Many factors play a role but people pleasing, low self-esteem and the inability to set boundaries are major causes.

Eventually, our black box of resentment explodes. We simply cannot take any more. Someone we care about deeply may set off this explosion and it could damage our relationship for years to come or it may even destroy it permanently. Another reason why people are unhappy is that we mould ourselves into who we are not because society expects us to behave in a certain way. Our pseudo persona of perfection begins to form as we mature and every time we are hurt or uncomfortable, this pseudo persona, or mask, grows another protective layer.

We begin to disappear behind this mask of perfection that we present to the world. Eventually, we begin to feel that no-one knows who we are and that no-one understands us. How can they really understand us if all we present to them is a mask of perfection? We created this mask to hide our pain and embarrassment from the world. We fear that if we show our true selves to the world, we will not be loved or accepted. By the time we are in our forties, this mask has become a familiar face, even to us, and *we* don't even know who we are anymore.

This is when we may have that dreaded mid-life crisis, which can manifest in many different ways. Perhaps we want a divorce or we buy a fancy sports car, or we focus on extreme fitness. In order to remove these masks and to live life more authentically, we need to find out who we really are. We need to remove the protective layers that we have created around our fragile hearts in order to live the life we really choose to live.

We cannot live an authentic life if we really do not know who we are. The only way to get back to authenticity is to examine every aspect of our lives. We need to analyse every belief system and everything we were taught as children. We need to decide what serves us and what no longer serves us.

Once we have done this and discarded all that no longer serves us, we can begin to focus on our true personality and leave the false personality, which is vested in pain and resentment, behind. We can then build a future on the solid foundation of our true personality, the part of each one of us that is linked to our heart and our soul. Life is easier without masks.

KARMA

31st July 2015

Karma is not a punishment in which others may revel at your expense. It is an agreement with your soul to experience opposites. Karma is duality in process.

CONSCIOUSNESS

3rd August 2015

No one can compel another to become more aware by using force. We can never force anyone else to see our point of view, not even if we threaten them with hellfire and brimstone. It would be as effective as squishing a peach to try and ripen it.

In my view of the world, consciousness evolves as we live each lifetime. Sadly, consciousness, like nature, evolves very slowly. It takes many lifetimes to learn things such as compassion, harmony, peace, love and joy.

Every one of us has experienced lifetimes of violence, destruction, corruption and hatred. Every one of us! This is how we learn to choose differently. It's impossible for us to understand any aspect of life if we have not experienced it ourselves. Every experience has two sides, a positive and a negative. If we look back on our lives, we clearly see that understanding and compassion only occur if we have had a similar experience as someone who is suffering. I, for example, though I behaved in a compassionate way towards people who lost a spouse, truly know that I was not as compassionate as I thought I was. I had no idea what it was like to lose a spouse. But now that I have lost a partner, I do understand, and I can truly empathise.

Therefore, if we encounter an individual who we deem to be a violent, mean, corrupt, enraged, racist, or whatever other judgment we might have, we may be outraged and shocked. We forget that we were once all of those things and may even be all of those things to a lesser degree in the future.

Perhaps we will do a better job in our lives if we lead by example, rather than make the so-called perpetrator wrong. Perhaps the world will be a better place if we teach the perpetrators that love is the only way. Perhaps, if we as a society bring understanding and compassion to the table instead of fear and hatred, our world will be a better place.

In ancient cultures, we displayed more compassion towards those who may not have been as evolved. The ancients knew that it took compassion and love to teach an individual to be respectful, kind, and loving. This could be made manifest by reminding a misbehaving child of who they really are when they have done something wrong or have made a mistake. Perhaps we can remind a child that they helped a neighbour the previous day. Or we could remind the child of other loving and kind things they have done in the past. By positive re-enforcement, we can uplift and change our world from critical and violent to accepting and loving.

In our world, we berate, judge, and punish those we see as different or less evolved than us. I wish I could be more compassionate and understanding of all life in the universe. Alas, I am simply not evolved enough to let go of all of my own judgments and fears. I am only just beginning to understand how my thoughts, words and deeds impact others and the world around me.

HANDING OUR PERSONAL POWER OVER TO OTHERS

26th August 2015

We become chained to beliefs that no longer serve us. We follow blindly where others lead without deciding for ourselves what serves *us*. We accept the standards that others set for beauty, peace, love, and happiness. Education, media, society, and others who influence our lives imprint these standards on us.

We seldom have the courage to stop for a minute and ask, "What would love do?" and, "Who does it serve?" Imagine if we asked ourselves those two questions before we made any life decisions. We blame the devil or anything else that we can blame, for everything that goes wrong, and we assign credit to God, the Universe, or someone else, for everything that goes right.

We are conscious beings, made in the image of the Divine. We and we alone decide what is right and what is wrong. To blame, conform, rejoice, love, or do anything by anyone else's standards *does not* serve us! Wake up to your *own* power.

We all have an inner barometer of right and wrong, good and evil, happy and sad, beautiful and ugly. Follow your *own* barometer. Take your power back. We know that when we do something wrong or hurtful that we are doing so because we *feel* it inside.

We know when we do something right or loving because we feel it inside as well. Do more of what makes you feel good inside. That which makes us feel good inside is that which emanates from the Divine. Do more of that.

CORRUPTED MESSAGES

7th September 2015

The King James version of the New Testament was completed in 1611 by eight members of the Church of England. There were, and still are, no original texts to translate. The oldest manuscripts we have were written down hundreds of years after the last apostle died. There are over 8000 of these old manuscripts, with no two alike.

The King James translators used none of these anyway. Instead, they edited previous translations to create a version that their kin and parliament would approve of.

Therefore, 21st century Christians believe the *Word of God* is a book edited in the 17th Century from 16th Century translations of 8000 contradictory copies of 4th-century scrolls that claim to be copies of lost letters written in the first century.

That is not faith. That is insanity. All messages can, and often do, become corrupted - broken telephone for sure! How can you be sure you are practising correct principles, irrespective of your religious orientation? If what you're doing or saying comes from a place of love, honour, and respect, you're doing okay. Leave God or the Universe, the Light, science or any other higher power you wish to invoke, or whose approval you seek, out of it.

If you let your inner guidance system lead you, you can't really go wrong. From my perspective, there is no reward or punishment that anyone *out there* can inflict on you. All religions, if you whittle them down to their basic tenets, teach love. We are hard-wired to seek love. I'm not talking about romanticised love. I'm talking Agapé - unconditional love.

None of us can really even understand what that means, because we simply cannot put our heads around love that is without any judgement or conditions. In the last few weeks, I have read so many messages on social media that refer to *my God,* or the *one true path*, or accepting one philosophical/religious view as the only way. Divine intelligence, no matter what you call it, whether that is God, Buddha, Mohammed, science, quantum mechanics, nature, pure physics, or any other thing that can astound us, is way too intelligent to give us just one point of view.

DON'T SWEAT THE SMALL STUFF

12th September 2015

So often we throw out these statements without really under-standing the true meaning. Let me tell you what you will miss when those you love are no longer there.

You will *wish* they could stomp dirt onto the kitchen floor. How you will miss that the toilet seat is up – again. You will smile wistfully at the thought of the toilet paper being put on the wrong way around. You will regret the time you said no, whether that was for a quickie, a kiss, or listening again to his or her old, tired jokes. You will miss the messy kitchen and wish you could complain about the long grass.

You will miss times you were unhappy that they spent too much time with their friends, watching sport, reading, or listening to the same song. You will miss the underwear lying on the floor. You will regret that you did not say, "I love you," more often. You will regret your harsh words. You will regret that you did not support their crazy ideas. You will spend a great deal of time wondering why all these little things seem so important now. It is only when we lose someone to death that we really truly understand what we had.

Here is what I know to be true: If you love him or her, tell them

– often. Don't speak to them like you're their parent. This is a much bigger problem than you think. I often cringe at how spouses speak to each other.

That which you require of them, first do and be that yourself. When they *misbehave*, remind them that this is not who they truly are. Remind them that you know who they truly are, and you know who the real person is that you love and have always loved. If you see only that which is good and fine in your partner, they will show you more of that. Mind your words, they will cause most of your regrets.

DOUBLE STANDARDS – WE CAN'T WIN

19th September 2015

If you eat cake – you're damaging your health

If you drive a big car – you're damaging the environment

If you print that email – you're destroying the rain forest

If you don't love my God – you're definitely going to my hell

If you don't wear what's in fashion – you will be judged

If you have too much money – you're selfish and greedy

If you have too little money – you're lazy and uninspired

If you eat butter instead of coconut oil – you're not paying attention

If you don't eat organic – you will die

If you are black - you're a criminal

If you are white - you're a racist

If you are too thin – you are just showing off

If you are too fat – you lack willpower

If you don't have the right phone – you lack taste

If you don't pick a side – you're not committed

If you wear leather – you're inhumane

If you don't share a photo – you have no heart

If you like knitting – you must be old fashioned

If you don't meditate this way – you're doing it wrong

If I don't make this list longer – someone will be upset

None of it is relevant or true. For as long as we are at war with each other in this way, there can be no peace on earth. All judgement does is cause more strife and division. The bigger the strife, the more people fall into the trap of that judgement, and the more hectic the conflict. People die because of our judgements. Wars are created over it.

Judge less. Love more. It will change your life! Just allow everyone to find their own way to love, God, happiness or truth. It will make the world a better place.

I REMEMBER A TIME

5th October 2015

I remember in the past, we were not ill all the time. I remember growing all our own vegetables. I remember getting our milk from the local farmer. I remember a time when we had chickens to provide us with eggs and meat, all in our suburban back yard. I remember when we ate what was in season when things did not have to be flown halfway around the world.

I remember a time when I had two pairs of shoes, one pair for home and school and one pair for going out. I remember a time when I had enough clothes for *one* week. Not more clothes than I could ever possibly wear. I remember a time when neighbours knew each other and helped out - often. I remember a time when we were respectful of the beliefs of others. I remember a time when family really mattered. I remember a time when all the children could play outside.

Perhaps I remember it wrong. Perhaps the past was also as messed up in its own way. But today, we live in a fast-paced, consumer society, driven by instant gratification. I remember that I used to wait in anticipation for the mulberries to ripen. I remember all the neighbourhood children coming to eat their fill from our tree. I remember having our own fruit trees and there was so much fruit that my mother made her own jam and preserves. And yes, she had a full-time job. I remember a time when supermarkets closed at noon on Saturday and nobody starved. The staff could at least spend some time with their families.

The biggest impact we have on the planet is not what we eat, what chemicals we use, or how we pray, it's what we consume. It is amazing how often we criticise others for not believing as we believe, whether that is religion, diet, skin colour, weight or the right cell phone or sports shoes.

Worry more about our need to endlessly have more and more, and consume, consume, consume, than whether someone is worshipping the right God, or if someone is using cancer medication of which you do not approve. Worry more about being kind than being right. Worry more about love, than pointing out someone's failures. Worry more about what's in your heart than what surrounds you.

THE RULER AS A RELATIONSHIP TOOL

10th October 2015

Imagine that you have a 1-meter ruler and imagine that every millimetre of the 1000 millimetres on that ruler represents one issue in your relationship: Money, kitchen floor, car, job, lawn, and dishes. Each one of those is represented by a single millimetre on that ruler. Now, look at the number of times you became upset because of *one* issue - one millimetre.

When we focus on only one issue that irritates or angers us in our relationship, we allow that issue to cloud or drown out all the other 999 issues that may be *perfect* in this moment. Put the issues back in perspective and look at your *entire* relationship and decide again if it is worth destroying your whole relationship over *one issue*.

I love working with people to help them improve their relationships. Not just the romantic ones. The relationship you have with yourself defines the relationships you have with others. The entire world is a reflection of our relationships. Know who you are and what you want, and your life will change. Most of us really do not know who we are and over the years that I have been doing this work, very few people have been able to tell me what they want.

You can't get what you want if you do not know what it is. We often know what we don't want, yet very few of us are able to verbalise what we do want.

WHAT WOMEN REALLY WANT

13th October 2015

She needs to feel safe. Her home is her sanctuary. If it is not safe there, where must she go?

She needs your respect. There is enough disrespect in the world.

She needs to feel heard. If you do not understand her needs and desires, how would you know what keeps her content?

Be her go-to guy.

If she cannot share her fears with you, she probably does not feel safe.

If you bail out when times get tough, she will lose trust.

Be strong when it is called for.

Only one of us can fall apart at any given time.

Hormone jokes apply to testosterone as well.

Don't follow the masses... it shows you're a fool.

See that which is the best in her, and she will show you more of that.

Keep issues in perspective.

Don't allow little things to wreck a good relationship.

Be honest - always! Even when it is difficult. Yet, guard against making this honesty unkind.

Never, ever speak to her as if you are her parent. For when you do, she has no choice but to behave like a child.

Real love is all that matters. Love is a verb. You show your love by what you *do*, not what you say.

In return she will:

Make you feel safe

Respect you

Hear you

Be your go-to girl

Support you when times get tough

Be strong when you can't be

She will see past the testosterone moments

Keep issues in perspective

Be honest and kind

She won't treat you like a child

Real love is all that matters. Love is a verb. You show your love by what you *do*, not what you say.

LIFE...

17th October 2015

It has absolutely no meaning or purpose other than that which *you* give it! You are the Universe expressing itself.

CREATE A BOND OF RESPECT AND TRUST

18th October 2015

I recently ran a small relationship survey on social media, asking people what they thought was the most important requirement in their relationship. The results presented me with interesting data. I am by no means suggesting that this is a scientific breakthrough, considering my very small sample.

Trust and respect came out on top. When I conducted surveys at Namasté magazine, I found that once you have about 100 survey results, the percentages don't really change much after that, so I'll go with that as my measure.

I know and have known for a long time, that the way we conduct our relationships, both romantic and otherwise, does not work. And, if the most dominant requirement in our relationships seems to be respect and trust, how do we go about achieving that? I do believe that this subject will require a whole book and I intend to write that. But let me attempt to give you some ideas to ponder here.

Respect:

This is a very subjective matter. For me then, what does this mean? Respect is how I require you to treat me, how you speak to me, not just verbal communication but your body language as well. For example; if we were talking about something that is my passion, I know that this is not necessarily your passion. But I want you to really hear me. We often share something with our spouses, family or friends and we are completely aware that the party to whom we are speaking is not listening. Or they may roll their eyes while we are talking. Not only is this passive aggressive behaviour on some subliminal level, (and sometimes not so subliminal), it makes us feel disrespected as well.

It makes us feel as if our opinions don't count and we feel marginalised. This seems such a small thing and it is a very insignificant example. But it serves to make us understand that respect is not always about the big things. If you understand what constitutes respect for the person with whom you are interacting, you will have a better relationship with them. Spend some time asking anybody with whom you interact what it is that you do that makes them feel respected or disrespected. If you know the answer to these questions, your relationships will improve, provided that the relationships are important enough for you to choose to change your behaviour so that your interaction with those around you becomes more respectful.

Trust:

Every one of us has experienced betrayal. Betrayal has many faces. Our brain will take our past experiences and super-impose that experience on our current situation. Very often, it is our anticipation that the past experience will repeat itself that causes us to react to the current situation with past vehemence.

Having said that, our partner may not really understand our past experiences and may be oblivious to the reason why we are reacting as we are. I'll give you an example. In my past, I was in a violent marriage. My past experience associates loud male voices and the use of tools, like a drill or a screwdriver, with this violent memory. In my relationship with Roy, almost every time he worked with tools of any description, or if he spoke in a loud voice, I would withdraw. I withdrew in anticipation of imminent violence. His interpretation of my withdrawal was that I was not willing to help him. This caused conflict in our relationship until I had the courage to explain my past experience and could trust him that he would take my explanation seriously. He did.

Each time he started working with tools, he made sure that his voice was on an even keel and when he picked up a tool and noticed that I had withdrawn, he would come and to me and say something like, "I love you, I will never hurt you. You are safe. Come and help me." It took a huge level of trust to make myself this vulnerable to him, and once I became honest about my past, I could create a different experience. The change was incredible. Once I opened up and became honest about my past and *my* issues, trust could be built between us. Slowly, I learned to trust again and replaced the trigger response of my past with a new experience that ensured a different future.

Think about respect and trust and find out what this means in *your* relationships. It seems to be of paramount importance to all of us.

LOVE VERSUS FEAR

19th October 2015

Many people think the opposite of love is hate, it is not, it is fear.

All emotions can be sorted into these two categories:

Under love, you will find emotions such as:

Joy, fun, compassion, humility, kindness, etc.

Under fear comes emotions such as:

Hate, anger, spite, judgment, etc.

This is an endless external and internal battle of good and evil, right and wrong, yin and yang, darkness and light, positive and negative, God and the devil or whatever you choose to call it.

We are hard-wired to seek love. In each of us resides an internal measure of this - we intuitively *know* the difference between love and fear. Our personality is also divided into these two categories. Our personality traits have positive aspects as well as negative aspects.

The positive aspects of our personality are linked to love/God/soul, or whatever you choose to call it. The negative aspects of our personality are linked to fear/devil/negativity, or whatever you wish to call it.

For me, it is not that we should deny or try to annihilate the negative aspects of who we are – we are both – love and fear. For me, it is becoming conscious of the dichotomy. This consciousness allows us to recognise when we are trapped in the negative aspect of who we are. When we become conscious, we can choose again and again who we want to be in every moment.

Our brain is hard-wired with this love/fear dynamic as well. This is a physiological fact! We are all hard-wired for flight/fight or freeze/fold. We all know what this feels like. When we are in flight/fight or freeze/fold mode, we are literally incapable of making loving and compassionate decisions.

There are tools to help us to extricate ourselves from this flight/fight, freeze/fold situation. Once we are able to get our autonomic nervous system back in balance, we release our body from its flight/fight; freeze/fold prison and we can engage our heart centre once more. The world around us is a reflection of this. As above, so below. As within, so without.

The conflict in the world is a reflection of the conflict in each and every one of us. Once we become aware that we are trapped in the negative aspect of our personality, we can apply a simple meditative tool to help us get back into the love aspect or positive aspect of who we are.

This eternal external, internal battle rages on in each one of us and it is this battle that makes our lives difficult. This battle never ceases completely, and when we learn to identify and then extricate ourselves from it, our lives and relationships become much more peaceful. We learn who we truly are – that part of us that is eternally linked to our soul/God/love.

We are not that which is governed by fear. We are love and we have always been love, trapped in a body that is governed by the flight/fight, freeze/fold dynamic.

We can choose again - in every moment of every day - we can choose again who we want to be and how we wish to react in any situation.

THERE IS ENOUGH

21st October 2015

There are enough resources on this planet for *everyone* to have their basic needs of food, shelter, and clothes, met. *Everyone*! We have allowed our idea that there is not enough and, therefore, that we must hoard, to take control of our capacity for compassion. It is a basic human right to have one's basic needs met. This will never detract from those who choose to have more than just the basics.

When did we begin to make it okay to pay our movie and sports stars an obscene amount of money, while our nurses and teachers live on, or below, the poverty line? When did we begin to make it okay that our religious institutions become some of the richest organisations in the world and we continue to hear of atrocities perpetrated by them? When did we stop caring for and about our neighbours?

When did we decide that those who work for the good of others, such as NGOs, must earn just enough, or even below, the poverty line and when did we start criticising them with statements like, "You're just in it for the money?" We *know* that most of the people who work for non-profit organisations do so because it is a heart-breaking task. I have yet to meet someone who works for a non-profit organisation because of the financial rewards it offers. When we see those people driving a nice car, we immediately judge them! When did we decide that they should not be well rewarded for their efforts?

Those silent supporters of the world, teachers, nurses, carers for the aged, cleaners, and all others who work tirelessly behind the scenes, I love you and thank you. Thank you for making the world a better place. You are the blood that courses through the veins of our world.

When did we begin to idolise those who have more than they will ever need - for generations to come - but we neglect those who are changing the world? Those who are making a difference in the lives of others deserve so much more than we give them.

FROM YOUR HEART

24th October 2016

In everything you do, let it emanate from your heart. If your heart is involved, it will make you feel better about who you are, and you will change the world. Every time. Your heart knows what your head cannot even imagine.

BALANCE

26th October 2015

Sadly, most of us believe that if we practise good spiritual deeds, whatever that may mean to us, we are on the *right path* and often we make our right path the one and only true path. Whether we believe in the teachings of Buddha, Jesus, Mohammed, Kali, God, or any other deity, the teachings are essentially the same; Love.

Spiritual practise is indeed extremely valuable. Never stop your spiritual practise. Our energy system, however, is designed in such a way that our spiritual practise is balanced with our physical practise. The heart chakra is what interlocks the two. There are three chakras, or energy vortices, above our heart chakra and three below. The top three relate to our spiritual self and the three below the heart chakra relate to our physical self. If our energy system is out of balance in either the physical aspect or the spiritual aspect, our lives will also be out of balance.

If we are only nurturing our top three chakras, our spiritual self, with spiritual practise and neglecting the bottom three chakras, our physical self, our lives will not work as well as we would like them to. To deny the physical aspect of our nature is as detrimental to us as denying our spiritual aspect. Both work together with the heart chakra as the focus, or connection point.

An example: If we focus predominantly on spiritual practise by means of prayer, religion, meditation, chanting, or other spiritual practise, our top three chakras will be better developed. Very often we make others' spiritual practise wrong, because it is different from our own and, by this very act, we negate most of the benefits of our own spiritual practise.

By the same token, if we focus predominantly on our physical aspect, the bottom three chakras will be out of balance with the top three chakras.

The heart, of course, is where the link resides. Our belief systems reside there. If we deny any aspect of our physicality or any aspect of our spirituality, or if we judge something to be wrong or unacceptable, our energy system will be out of balance irrespective of our practise.

Therefore, we should look into our hearts and see what resides there. If spite, anger, judgment, or racism resides in our hearts, this is the energy we will send into the world and the world will reflect that energy back to us. If, on the other hand, compassion, acceptance, love, and joy reside in our hearts, then that will also be the energy we send out into the world and the world will reflect that energy back to us. We experience what we believe to be true and our outer world is a reflection of our inner world.

Example: We cannot expect to experience world peace if we are constantly fighting with our spouse, children, neighbours, or whomever. We cannot expect religious tolerance if we make the religious practise of anyone else wrong.

Just as our bodies' energy system reflects our reality, so our collective energy systems reflect the reality in our world.

FIGHTING AND RESISTANCE DON'T WORK

28th October 2015

No one can *resist* something in the hope of change. No one can *fight* something in the hope of change. No one can be *against* something in the hope of change.

Only love, acceptance, education, and persuasion can change anything. And the greatest of these *is Love*.

Any change will only occur if we lead by example. However, resistance, fighting and being against something is a great way to bring it into consciousness.

GOD DOES NOT CHOOSE PEOPLE. PEOPLE CHOOSE GOD

31st October 2015

God. Spirit. The Universe. It does not matter by what name you call that which you consider Divine. That which is divine has no need for you to believe in it - or even acknowledge it. It is a little like photosynthesis. A leaf does not have to believe in photosynthesis to turn green. Photosynthesis has no desire that anyone believes in its existence. It just is. It is a problem for me that people believe God has an ego. This is not true.

How can we then suggest that God chooses good behaviour over *bad* behaviour? One of our holy books says, "There is nowhere that I am not." If we start changing our enforced belief system that God is an authoritarian Caucasian male with a huge ego, who insists on ten rules, the world will be a better place.

Sadly, history shows us that many people have died in the name of God because *we* believe that *our* idea of God is the right and only true one and that this belief somehow gives us the right to make another's idea of God wrong!

This is so very deeply sad. Killing in the name of God is, for me, the ultimate blasphemy. God=Love and Love=God. We need more love, not judgement and disagreement.

ANIMALS TEACH US ABOUT UNCONDITIONAL LOVE

2nd November 2015

This is true. Imagine then, if we learned from them and treated each other with as much love, tolerance, and patience. We are much more patient with our animals than we are with our spouses. We forgive our animals much more readily than we forgive our spouses, friends, family, and children.

We rise up as one to defend animal rights, yet we often fail to rise up *for* child safety or spousal respect. We seldom rally *against* the atrocities of war.

We tolerate snippy behaviour from our animals much more than we would from our loved ones. We handle our animals' off days with more compassion than we would the people we love.

I can only imagine how I'd react if my partner unrolled the toilet paper seven times a week. I know how I have reacted in the past when my partner broke my special vase or scratched my car. I know that I'd get irritated if my partner vomited up a hairball on my rug every other week. Yes, animals do teach us unconditional love, we just fail to learn from them.

GENDER BASHING

6th November 2015

I find it bizarre that we anticipate being in harmonious, loving, and happy relationships if we continue to make the other gender *wrong* or inferior. I'm so bored with the PMS jokes and the battle of the sexes in particular. I'm even more bored with how we depict men as helpless when it comes to raising children or cooking, or other household chores.

We are all governed by chemistry. Hormones affect everyone. Just think how much chaos has been caused by testosterone. It is no different from oestrogen. If it is out of balance, we're pretty much stuffed.

Once we understand that men and women are different by design, we may begin to celebrate the differences and perhaps we can learn to live in peace with each other.

The world reflects our state of consciousness. Our consciousness is the microcosm of the macrocosm. How we behave in the world is how the world becomes. How can we possibly expect to live in a peaceful world if we cannot live in peace with each other?

IT'S ALL ABOUT THE HEART

4th November 2015

If our hearts have shut down, we are bankrupt. It does not matter how much money we have.

KARMA - ONE OF THE MOST MISUNDERSTOOD CONCEPTS

7th November 2015

If we believe that karma is a fair punishment for wrong deeds, then we have not moved any further from the out-dated belief in heaven and hell. It is still reward/punishment. All we have done is change the words. Hell: punishment from a higher power for deeds we consider wrong. We are normally threatened with heaven and hell by people who believe that their idea of right and wrong is correct.

Karma: fair punishment for past behaviour, which is usually promoted by someone who believes that another got what he or she deserved because of some perceived wrongdoing.

Try telling someone whose son was just killed by a wild animal, or someone who has just been brutally raped, that "Karma is a bitch."

Conscious evolution demands love, compassion and understanding. Life is hard enough; we need never revel in the pain of others. We are all at different levels of our own evolutionary process. We all have past karmic ribbons. Perhaps we can look at those who we deem *wrong* and instead say something like, "There but for the grace of time/God/The Universe, go I".

I truly believe that we have sacred contacts with other souls who agree that we learn about a concept in tandem with each other. Learning is experiencing the positive and the negative of any experience. We interact with the same souls until we have understood and become neutral about a concept. Mastery is achieved once we have become neutral about a subject, and great compassion is shown to souls who are still learning about something that we have reached neutrality about. I believe that this is how we make our way back to Agapé, or unconditional love.

AS ABOVE, SO BELOW. AS WITHIN, SO WITHOUT

14th November 2015

It is so sad that the disagreements between friends about who's right and who's wrong are so prolific. And who's at fault and who must be punished, and that self-righteous religionists, conspiracy theorists, and scaremongers are the order of the day. Ultimately, this is exactly why the world is in such a state. Our small-minded bickering amongst each other is no different from one country declaring war on another. The scale is just a tad bigger.

I wish we could all just come to a space of peace in our own hearts. Perhaps if those of us who meditate and can manage to stay calm, do what we can to calm those around us, it may make a difference.

Hatred begets hatred, fear begets fear. Love begets love. *All* religions teach love as their primary focus. The hatred and discontent are a function of our ego and our need to be right and have absolutely nothing to do with anything we may consider divine.

I will continue to focus on peace, compassion and love.

YOUR SOUL CANNOT BE DAMAGED

11th December 2015

Your soul is perfect and has nothing to learn, be, or do. You cannot sell it, give it away, or harm it in any way. Your soul is eternal and is part of the ultimate consciousness, or God. It is the part of you that is forever and will be forever. Your consciousness can keep you trapped in a belief system that convinces you otherwise. There is neither reward nor punishment - it simply *is*.

Everything you experience on earth is your consciousness experiencing duality. Your soul has no ego and, therefore, has no requirement for you to be, do or have anything. You have chosen this physical life in order to know what love is not, and then to find your way back to love. For without darkness, you cannot perceive light. Without fear, hate, and discontent, you cannot perceive love, joy and harmony.

Your soul is part of what I call the *Realm of the Absolute* and everything that emanates either from the positive or the negative, expands the Realm of the Absolute. We choose whether we expand using the mechanism of love, or we expand using the mechanism of fear. Either way, knowledge and experience are gained and the Realm of the Absolute expands. The Realm of the Absolute, or God, has no ego and therefore, has no judgment that something is either good or bad, it simply is, and accepts everything as expansion or experience. It is easier for us if we use the mechanism of love.

RESENTMENT AND PARENTING YOUR PARTNER

18th December 2015

Over the years, I have coached many people seeking better relationships and found that it is almost always the same stuff that is destroying our relationships. Here are three of the biggest relationship destroyers:

1) Resentment:

We all get resentful. We could feel that we are carrying the bulk of the relationship burden - it rarely matters what the actual burden is. It could be as large as being the sole breadwinner, or the fact that we make the coffee most often. Resentment is rarely voiced and, if it is voiced, it is often done in a confrontational and accusatory way.

Learn to clear your black box of resentment in a safe, kind, and constructive way. When we feel heard, our resentments dissipate. If we do not clear the little resentments regularly, our black box of resentment gets so full that a minor event may cause the built-up pressure of resentment to explode. This is often evidenced when we seemingly overreact to something small. It is not a particular *event* to which we are over-reacting, it's a whole series of built-up little resentments that cause the explosion.

2) Being the Parent:

I am often astounded at how spouses speak to each other. An example of parent mode could be, "Why do you always have to....?" Or, "Why must I always...?" One clear indication that a spouse is in constant parent mode, is if I hear someone say something like, "My husband is like a child." I can almost guarantee that parent mode has taken control of this relationship. This is a very big problem.

If either spouse is constantly in parent mode, the other has no choice but to be either in *rebellious child* or *withdrawn child* mode. This is a vicious cycle that never serves the relationship. Learn how to communicate with each other as adults.

3) Not Knowing Who You Truly Are:

Over the years we have built up masks to protect ourselves from pain. These masks are not who we really are. We almost lose our true, authentic self to this protective mask. Yet, this mask is how we present ourselves to the world and this is who our potential new partner meets and interacts with.

While our authentic self hides behind the safety of this mask, we will never have a truly fulfilling relationship. Because of this mask, we have no real idea about what it is we want. How can we? If we have forgotten who we really are, how can we possibly know what we truly need in any of our relationships?

We take the same old dysfunctional stuff into our new relationships and we are astounded that the new relationship ends in the same way as all our past relationships. That's just crazy. If we want a different relationship, we have to change the way we behave within our relationships. Our habitual negative behaviour patterns often become so ingrained, that we are not even able to recognise them.

We can only truly have great relationships when we know who

we are: our true authentic self. When we know who we are, we can begin to define what we really need to feel loved, safe, and nurtured.

The trick, of course, is to understand that not all of us need the same things in order to feel loved, safe and nurtured.

NEW YEAR'S WISH

1st January 2016

I wish that I do not impose my beliefs on others.

I wish to be free of racism.

I wish to be less judgmental about the lifestyle choices of others.

I wish to be accepting of everyone's sexual orientation.

I wish to be more considerate of the pain others feel.

I wish to be courteous to those who work long hours behind tills.

I wish to open my heart to those in need.

I wish for peace in my heart and the world.

I wish to be kind to those who are battling with life.

I wish to be truthful in my dealings with others.

I wish to be patient around those who are old and frail.

I wish to be a better person than I was last year.

I wish for love to be present in everything I do. May the coming year be filled with love.

I BELIEVE IN RE-INCARNATION

4th January 2016

That means that I have been a man, woman, transvestite, gay, lesbian, black, white, Greek, Chinese, French, Zulu, American, Ethiopian, Polish, English, rich, poor, drunk, addict, prostitute, priest, saviour, murderer, hijacker, veteran, housewife, con-artist, prisoner, guard, saint, and any other thing one could possibly imagine.

I also understand that we incarnate on this planet to learn how to love everything about this planet. And this planet is certainly not the only one on which we have had an opportunity to incarnate.

I believe, as well, in the evolution of consciousness, and that consciousness is energy. In my view of the world, this would mean that as you experience each life, so your level of consciousness and understanding, or energy, increases.

That which we call God is all the energy that exists in its infinity. I believe that we, and everything in the universe, are an expression of that energy, or consciousness. In one of our holy books, and there are many, it says, "There is nowhere that I am not."

It does not matter to me which holy book you're currently in favour of since that would depend upon where you've chosen to incarnate in this lifetime, and the influence your current society has upon your life.

It doesn't matter to me which skin colour you have chosen this lifetime. It doesn't matter to me what language you speak. It doesn't matter to me the colour or shape of your eyes.

As far as I understand it, I believe that the universe, or energy, or consciousness, continues to move towards greater and greater complexity, with God being the ultimate complexity. (Thank you, Gregory David Roberts, author of *Shantaram*). We then have the choice to either contribute to the movement towards greater complexity, which is the path of love and acceptance, or we inhibit the movement towards greater complexity, which is the path of fear, hate, and judgment.

Again, I can only say that I aspire to reach a state of complete and unconditional love. If I manage it for 30 seconds longer today than I did yesterday, I'm moving in the direction towards ultimate complexity or Agapé - love without condition, judgment or need.

In my view of the world, all the stuff that offends us then becomes obsolete. I wish for peace and love in the world.

THERE IS ALWAYS A CHOICE

5th January 2016

One Chooses to be Kind.

If one's kindness is dependent on the appreciation of others, then it's not kindness that emanates from our very being. It is window dressing.

One chooses integrity.

If one's integrity lasts only as long as others are honourable, we only pretend to have integrity.

One chooses love.

Choose love even if the people around one are not loving.

It is our inability to set boundaries that brings this into conflict. Being these things consistently should not be dependent on others and their behaviour. Few of us know how to state clearly, and in a kind and loving way, what we need within any relationship in order for us to remain kind, honourable and loving.

We allow little resentments to go unspoken and this builds up and causes us to be less loving, kind and honourable. We can't possibly know how to set boundaries if we don't know who we truly are. The masks we are wearing that we put there because of our past painful experiences have become part of our *normal* persona. Yet, we still feel lost, unloved, unheard, and unappreciated. That is because our true self is in hiding.

RIPPLE EFFECT

6th January 2016

You are the stone falling in the pond of your life. Every decision you make and every action you take has a ripple effect, not just on you and your life and everyone in your circle, it ripples through the universe. The world is a reflection of our collective thoughts, words and actions.

Imagine that!

IT IS WHAT IT IS

10th January 2016

In every culture, within every race, within every religion, within every tribe, and within every nationality, there will be those who judge. We all judge. We look at those who are not as smart as we are, not a rich, not as poor, not as glamorous, not as stylish, not as open-minded, not as white, not as black, not as thin, not fat enough, not as heterosexual, not as feminine, not as masculine, and whatever else *not-as* that we can think of, and we judge it as unacceptable.

It is rare that we find ourselves without any judgement and, in my opinion, it is only those who have already achieved mastery, who cease to judge. I have yet to meet one person who has achieved mastery.

We have taken a few of these judgements and made them a national sport. We have taken racism, sexism, religion and our political viewpoint and we have decided that we feel so strongly about our points of view that we are threatening to kill each other over them. How is it possible in the 21st century that we are still unable to allow others to have a point of view that differs from ours?

Judgment fuels the fires of hatred and discontent. Let's try not to be so offended or so judgmental. Let's open our minds and hearts and begin to understand that people judge. It is unlikely that we will stop our own judgments. If we begin to understand that we judge just as much as the next person, we will begin to have compassion with each other because we will *know* that we are just a primitive race of people, who are like a pimple on the backside of the Universe and that none of it really matters.

All we can do is attempt to understand and out-grow our own judgments. If we understand that people say and do things because of who they are, and that it is our reaction to those things that creates the emotional tennis match, then let's just stop hitting the ball back.

May compassion, understanding and patience awaken the love inside each one of us!

THE DIFFERENCE BETWEEN AN EVENT AND A STORY

13th January 2016

An event is something that happened to you that you can do nothing about.

Example:

An Event: I had a car accident.

A Story: I had a car accident and I had to battle with service providers who were incompetent, the insurance company that was unhelpful, and the other driver who was an ignorant fool.

It is the *story* that we tell ourselves that makes life difficult. It is the story that holds us ransom to the event. It is the story that makes us a victim. Everyone has a story. Not everyone chooses to rise above it. Watch that you do not repeatedly tell your *story*. This only turns it into a pain party with your friends.

In this way, our consciousness affects our reality, the reality that exists on the planet, and how we create our view of the world. I understand that there are different scales of events. Breaking a nail is not the same as losing a partner. Be discerning! Get help if you need to.

Dealing with some events is really difficult and can take a long time to process. Allow yourself that time to heal.

Let's watch ourselves that we do not repeatedly tell our tragic story for the sake of telling it. If your story does not assist others in dealing with their story, if it is simply told to let others know how you have suffered, it does not serve anyone, least of all you.

WHAT WE THOUGHT WAS TRUE

22nd January 2016

Almost everything they taught us last century about health and well-being has been proven wrong. Not a day goes by that I do not see more and more articles about the dangers of this and an overturned decision about that.

My recommendation? Do what you feel is right. My Father smoked 90 cigarettes a day and drank himself into a stupor. My Mom was a teetotaller, who never smoked, drank or swore, and lived a clean and healthy lifestyle. She was a nurse. She died at 48. My Father died at 72. They died many years apart and both died as a result of motor car accidents.

My Gran ate everything she could lay her hands on, which included a lot of starch and a great deal of sugar. She lived to a ripe old age of 93 and she was always as skinny as a rake. I believe that when it is your day to die, it is your day to die. I also believe our ancestors were right: do and eat everything, but do it in moderation.

Roy was fit and healthy and had been for a medical check-up a few months before he died. The doctor told him his heart was as strong as an ox's. Yet, he died of a massive heart attack within months of that doctor's visit.

I believe if it is your day, it is your day. What I learned is that it is important to focus on the love, joy, and happiness in our lives rather than what we eat or what we own.

AGE AND AGEING

24th January 2016

I see and feel the benefit of having a positive attitude. And I know that when our attitude is positive, we do seem to look and feel better as we age. I understand that a healthy and active lifestyle seems to slow the ageing process. I also observe that genetics plays a major part in how we look and feel as we age.

Having said that, age is not something anybody can avoid. Birth and death are the cycle of life and are unavoidable. Age seems to be just another mechanism we use to judge ourselves and others. I love being my age. I love the freedom it brings. I love that I no longer have to worry what others think of me. I love that I no longer need to be so competitive. I love that I can look at the young people with fond memories of a time when I had such a lovely body.

I wish I knew then what I know now. I would not have been so shy. I would have been more courageous. I would have taken more chances. I would have worried less about the opinions of others. I would have travelled more and worried about money later. I would have loved more, laughed more, played more, worked less, shared more, and had a lot more fun.

I believe that I did more of those things than most of my peers.

Yet, looking back, I took life way too seriously. Opinions of others mattered too much. Before you know it, your children will be adults with their own lives. While you are raising them, never ever forget that you also have a duty to yourself as well. Don't forget to nurture yourself. Do the things you love.

Most important of all, do not sacrifice your relationship with your partner for the sake of anything. Do not let your parenting responsibilities, your job or your family override the importance of your relationship with your partner.

The biggest gift you can give your children is to love and respect their other parent.

FINDING A NEW WAY

28th January 2016

If you desire a relationship that works, I propose a new way. Instead of making a list of what you desire in a partner, why don't you say who *you* choose to *be* within a relationship and your partner will mirror that? I know it works. I have lived it! This is who I choose to be within my relationship.

1. I will not behave as though I am your parent. This means that I will never treat you like a child or make you feel like one.

2. I will tell you what makes me happy - often - because if you know what makes me happy, you will do more of that. This means that I will not *pick* at your negative behaviour. I will remind you gently of that part of you that I love.

3. I will keep things in perspective. This means that as the trivial things crop up, I will constantly ask myself if it is worth destroying our relationship over these issues, such as clothes lying about. If I understand your little quirks and look at them with humour, you will honour me with the same understanding.

4. I want the freedom to pursue the things I love, even if you choose not to participate. I would hope that you have interests that engage you as well, even if I choose not to participate.

5. Only one of us can fall apart at any given moment. If you fall apart, I want you to know that I will have your back without criticism or judgment.

6. I know you can't read minds. Neither can I. I will not play mind games.

7. I will not manipulate you. If I do, I'd like you to gently point that out to me.

8. I choose not to participate in jokes about how good/bad men/women are. It is challenging enough having a good relationship without still contributing to the battle of the sexes. The battle of the sexes only serves to distance us from each other and brings no honour.

Now that I know that a relationship like this is possible, I will not settle for less. Once we become conscious of our habitual negative behaviour patterns and how they affect our relationships, we can begin to work towards changing what no longer serves us.

INNER PEACE AND WORLD PEACE

6th February 2016

If we cannot live in peace and harmony with those we claim to love, how can we possibly expect world peace? A change from fear, war, and hatred, to love, compassion and joy begins at home. If we do not have it within us, we cannot find it without.

HABITUAL NEGATIVE BEHAVIOUR PATTERNS

10th February 2016

None of your relationships will change if you do not change your habitual, negative behaviour patterns. These form as a defence mechanism to past painful experiences. If you take the same old and tired behaviour patterns into a new relationship, the new relationship will just end like all the previous ones.

Once you are able to recognise your own habitual negative behaviour patterns, you can learn to move towards the positive aspects of who you truly are - your authentic self, not the individual who is guarded and jaded by past experience. When you connect to your authentic self, you will attract fulfilling, lasting and loving relationships.

HOW DO WE CHANGE THE WORLD?

15th February 2016

Be kind - irrespective of the nastiness of others.

Be thoughtful - irrespective of the inconsideration of others.

Be accepting - irrespective of the judgment of others.

Be loving - irrespective of the hatred in another's heart.

Be giving - irrespective of the miserliness of others.

Be compassionate - irrespective of the callousness of others.

We decide how we want to be in the world and that which we send out reflects back to us. What do you wish to see in your world mirror?

KNOWING THE DIFFERENCE BETWEEN REMORSE AND GUILT

16th February 2016

Remorse is something we feel when we believe we have done something that may have hurt or upset someone else. Remorse is what we feel when we truly regret something we have done.

Guilt, on the other hand, is something someone else wants us to feel. Often used as a form of emotional blackmail, we get caught in its mindless trap. Guilt is a completely wasted emotion.

Ask yourself, "Do I have something to feel remorseful about?" That will normally clear up any confusion.

TO ALL THE WOMEN I KNOW

20th February 2016

We are our own worst enemy. We have so many body issues because *we* promote them. We seem to be in constant competition with each other. We judge other women on their hair, the clothes they wear, the size of their boobs and their weight. We judge other women if we think they are too fat, or too skinny, too smart, or not smart enough.

We make statements such as, "She is too fat, old, tall, short, black, white to wear that." We make each other feel small, rather than build each other up. If a woman drives a nice car, we assume her husband bought it for her. If she has an impressive job, we wonder with whom she slept to get it.

How often do we call a company and ask for a manager and expect the more senior person to be male? We talk about women with curves as being better than a skinny woman, or the other way around.

How often do we hear one woman call another woman a bitch or a slut?

We make women not okay. Women are the guardians of society. *We* set the tone for what is acceptable and what is not. The men simply follow our lead. I am aware that not all women do this, but it's astounding how many play this demeaning game.

Isn't it time we gave that up? If we want equality and fairness, isn't it time we treated each other with a bit more respect? I rarely see men having a go at other men! It does happen and when it does, it's seldom about a man's body image.

Let's just stop being so mean, judgmental, and disrespectful to each other. How can we expect the world to respect and honour women if we do not practise what we preach? For a start, let's just become aware of how often these thoughts flit through our minds. That is where we start. Awareness.

THE TRANSITION INTO FULL OLD-SOUL CONSCIOUSNESS

25th February 2016

I have helped many old souls with their transition into full mani-festation of their *old-soul* consciousness. This transition is often fraught with chaos and confusion. It normally occurs as the person is approaching forty but can happen sooner, or even later, in life. I have seen this happen anywhere between 27 and 60 years of age. The transition into old soul consciousness can occur almost instantaneously, maybe when some life-altering event occurs, or it can be a slow process that could take years.

The manifestation of old soul consciousness occurs when the individual is no longer willing to live within the conflict of their current experience. It calls for the complete re-evaluation of who you believe you have been up to this point in your life, and who you choose to be, going forward. It's a time when we evaluate all our past experiences and discard the experiences and behaviours that no longer serve us.

This transition is often marked by severe emotional experiences, such as losing a job, home, financial security, or a traumatic divorce and, in many instances, a complete lifestyle change occurs. Perhaps you have practised as an accountant for most of your working career and you now feel unfulfilled and dissatisfied. This low-level dissatisfaction can seldom be quantified. You may even be aware that something is not right, but you may not have the words to adequately describe why you are dissatisfied.

No matter what sets this transition into motion, it may be traumatising for you. You may even put a lid on these feelings for a number of years. I have found that if we do not *pay attention* to the call of our souls, our highest self, God, the Universe will help us create an event that will push us over the edge. In my case, it was a very serious motorcar accident in which my son was involved. He nearly died as a result. This event made me take stock of my entire life. Nothing was the same for me after his accident. I wish I had a teacher who could have explained this process to me at the time.

I have had many minor *nudges* from my soul to re-evaluate and change my life, but I paid no attention. When we fail to pay attention to the little nudges, a *snot klap* (Bitch-slap, for my non-South African friends) event can occur, which will simply force us to acknowledge our new level of consciousness.

Change is inevitable. It can be a conscious transition, or it can be a transition that occurs by default. If it occurs by default, the chaos and confusion can be most debilitating. Help is available.

ANGER AND RAGE

28th February 2016

No one can do anything about the anger we carry inside us. The anger inside us belongs to no one but ourselves. Constant anger can be extremely debilitating. Constant anger stems from deeply buried feelings of inadequacy, resentment, and fear. Some of us are angry because we spilt a cup of tea. Others are angry because a partner may have ditched them. We are angry about abuse in all its forms, race, politics, animal abuse, child molestation, or whatever else we can be angry about. Some of us are even enraged by our outrage.

Irrespective of the reason for our anger and who is to blame for it, the anger still belongs to us. It resides in *our* hearts. I can do nothing about the anger in someone else's heart, even if they choose to hold on to it so tightly that they see nothing but their own rage and anger. I can only do something about the anger and rage in *my* heart. No one can help you get rid of your anger and if you are not willing to find a reason why you should release it, it will continue to rule your life.

As we all know, anger that lashes out creates more anger. Lashing out at another does not dissipate our anger. It neither decreases the anger in *our* hearts nor does it inspire love and compassion in the hearts of those against whom we are lashing out. The anger in our hearts can only begin to dissipate when we cease to be a victim of the event that caused the anger.

I am not suggesting by any stretch of the imagination that we are not entitled to feel anger. We are. Yet, we still have a choice to hang onto our anger and rage or to accept that we've had a raw deal and move into love. Anger and rage do not serve anyone. They are like a cancer that feeds on itself and grows but can never be sated.

I also have reasons to be angry and enraged. I lost my mother at an early age; my father was an alcoholic; I had a stepmother from hell; an uncle sexually molested me, and my husband beat me. I have been betrayed, hurt, beaten, abused and many other sad and unacceptable things. I can choose to be angry and I can allow my feelings of anger and rage to consume me.

The choice to hang onto our anger may even turn me into a perpetrator of the very things about which I am angry and outraged. Or, I can choose to replace the anger in my heart with love for myself, those around me and the world in general. I can acknowledge to myself that life was tough, and I can tell myself how brave I was to live through it. I can then replace that anger with deep honour and respect for myself because I have over-come the need to be a victim of my past. I can hold myself in high regard because I rose above my past and I can celebrate who I am now and who I am becoming.

Those who have had a challenging life have much to share with the world. How they choose to share the pain of their past is their choice. They can share the challenges of the past by projecting their anger and rage onto others and creating chal-lenges for them, or by teaching others that one can rise above the base anger and hatred of our past experiences and become an inspiration to others.

When we project our anger outward and cause others to be

angry and stir up hate, we are not serving ourselves, or anybody else. We are not making ourselves feel better, nor are we dissipating the anger and rage in our hearts. We are simply fuelling those fires of anger and rage, which will ultimately consume us completely. We will drag many others with us into our pit of anger and hate, so they too may begin to manifest anger and hate. Sometimes, this is the only way we think we can cope with our own rage and anger.

We can choose instead to release our own anger and we can decide that it no longer holds us in the grip of its power. While focusing on our rage and anger, we simply have no energy to create anything else. We never become aware of what may bring us love, peace, harmony and joy. If we are focused on our anger, we may not see the beautiful things as they show up in our lives. We shouldn't try to give up our anger for others, but for ourselves. Anger and rage never serve us. They keep us a prisoner of the event or events that caused it in the first place.

We all have reasons to be angry or filled with hatred. We can choose not to let it control everything that we think, say, and do. If we are not willing to give up our own inner anger and rage it will consume us, and it will most certainly consume our ability to feel joy.

We all have a choice.

DOES TIME REALLY HEAL US?

21st June 2016

When we have experienced trauma or loss, we know that time is what it takes to make us feel better. There is no telling how long it will take. It takes as long as it takes. More often than not, we put a lid on our pain and trauma, and we do not allow the pain to express itself. Inevitably, it will show itself.

When we suppress what we are feeling we just set ourselves up to feel those feelings at a later time. Something *will* trigger the need to express our pain. Do not hold back on honouring and expressing your emotional pain. Let it out. It is by letting it out that we allow ourselves to truly heal.

If we fail to express our feelings, they fester and boil inside us and this is how we become physically ill. Don't deny your feelings. Express them and do what you have to do to get to the other side of the storm. It is so liberating to let go and feel those feelings that we try so hard to deny.

It is through this process that we can begin to find peace once more. The only way to the other side is through the pain. I'm sending love and courage to all those facing and dealing with their inner turmoil.

CHOOSE TO LIVE AGAIN

13th July 2016

I believe that after deep trauma, one has to re-elect to be part of this thing called life. Yes, I know that the pain diminishes, and I know that people want you to move on.

None of it will matter unless and until you *choose* to live again. Breathing, eating, and going to work is not living. To live is to have meaning and purpose. After great trauma, meaning and purpose disappear. The loss is sometimes so great that the will to live no longer exists and after a great loss in my life, I often thought, "Oh no, I woke up. Again."

Know that you are on the mend when you begin to seek meaning and purpose once more. This is a slow process and can take time. We seem to live on *autopilot* for as long as it takes to process the trauma.

One fine day, we wake up and begin the act of redefining who we are now - our post-trauma self. I have asked myself who I am now. I am beginning to rediscover this new person emerging from the cocoon of trauma. I am deciding that I want to be here, on earth and alive. I am finding my new self and learning to fall in love with her and with life once more.

We can truly begin to heal when we can find a reason to get out of bed. That reason is never our ability to pay the rent or anything else as mundane. It is the meaning and purpose that we need in order to feel worthy and to feel as if we add value and that we *can* and *do* make a difference.

I am now searching once more for the mechanism by which I can fulfil my purpose and bring meaning to my life.

Take all the time that you need to recover after a traumatic experience. No one can tell you how long that will be. Often, we need help to find our own meaning and purpose once more. Hang in there. Just breathe.

WHAT DO WE NEED FROM RELATIONSHIPS?

16th July 2016

I had an opportunity recently to speak to a dear friend about relationships and what women need. We were sitting in his lovely house. I pointed out to him that modern women do not need what he has to offer.

He has a fabulous career, he can provide a comfortable lifestyle, and he is a *boy scout* and can fight off dragons. When I told him that I could do all those things for myself, he asked me, "Well, what do women want?"

From my perspective women are looking for emotional, physical, spiritual, and intellectual connection - c o n n e c t i o n. The poor man looked around in panic and he said something like... "I have been trained to be a provider. I have a house and a car and a cupboard full of groceries and I can protect my woman from harm. You are saying you do not need that."

With panic in his eyes, he said something like, "The cupboard that contains the stuff that you need is empty." He seemed almost in distress that he was now faced with a problem he could not solve. Men are problem solvers and doers, and he was stumped.

I think women need support, safety, harmony, and connection, not stuff and muscles. Since the emancipation of women, we have been able to procure all the material comforts ourselves.

The relationship paradigm has shifted. It has to be redefined. I love the way he could be honest about his fear. This paradigm shift made my friend understand that he now seemingly had nothing to offer a woman, and this made him feel inadequate, completely out of his depth, and vulnerable. We were both feeling vulnerable. Me, because I'm not used to asking for what I need, and he because he thought material possessions and protection from dragons is what women need. This is simply no longer true.

Men and women are now in the same position. We are aware that the way we conducted our relationships in the past is no longer working, but we don't really know how to change that. A consequence of this is that we rely on the battle of the sexes as our go-to response to any of our relationship issues. If we continue to blame the other gender for all the wrongs in our relationships, we don't have to change the way we conduct *ourselves* in the context of our relationships.

I have devised a way to redefine who we are in the context of our relationships. I shared this new way in my book, *Love Versus Fear*. It is the most vulnerable way of living that I have ever experienced, and it is so scary that it made my bones shake. But the rewards... Oh my God, the rewards are incredible! We *can* return to love, honour, respect, authenticity, joy, and hope.

MORE ON RELATIONSHIPS

18th July 2016

Are men feeling emasculated in today's emancipated society? Are women bone tired of trying to nurture their way back to love? Relationships are not about who pays the rent or who can afford to buy the bigger car or the fact that women can afford their own houses and cars.

It is no longer about old men with boats and the young women with whom they sail away. It is not about cougars and the young, strong, muscular body on her arm.

Yes, those relationships do exist, and they will continue to exist. But times have changed. A paradigm shift has occurred. What do we need from each other in the context of our most intimate relationships now, in this new paradigm?

Every time I post something on social media about relationships, the normal dead-end arguments come up. "I do so much for my man and he never appreciates it." Or, "Women only chase rich guys - they do not like nice guys." Yet, I see both genders posting gender jokes and sprouting vitriol about the other gender. We make fun of and are constantly disrespectful of each other. We whine and complain about what the other gender wants from us and how *they* should change to make *our* relationships better.

I have a friend who says he wants to be in a decent and loving relationship. Yet, he posts very misogynistic pictures on social media. When I pulled him up on it, he said, "I'm single, I can post what I want." This does nothing for his personal ethos and is indicative of what we do all the time.

We cannot make misogynistic and sexist comments and still expect to attract and conduct a loving and decent relationship in the long term. How do we fail to see the connection between our behaviour and the experience of our reality?

The fundamental way in which we conduct our relationships needs to change. I observe that most of us walk along the same blame-game, judgment, demand path, and expect our new relationships to somehow, by osmosis, produce different results.

If we do what we've always done, we will get what we've always got. The reality is that *very* few of our parents' relationships worked and very few of *their* parents' relationships worked. We model our current relationship dynamic on their experiences and methodologies. We are staring the obvious in the face and we fail to see that our relationships will continue to end the same way if we bring the same old, stale bullshit into the sacred relationship space.

Both genders are tired. It does not matter if you are in a homosexual or heterosexual relationship. We are tired. We are tired of the conflict. We are tired of the pain and we are tired of the loneliness. *We are tired.* We do not know how to live with each other, yet we yearn for connection, love, honour, and respect. There is another way. I know. I have lived it. And it is beautiful.

DIVINE MASCULINE AND DIVINE FEMININE

11th August 2016

Each one of us has both of these inside of us and both are needed in our world. Divine masculine is action driven, strong, outwardly focused, charges into *battle*, protects, leads, is intellectual, and has many other masculine traits.

Divine feminine is contemplative, flexible, inwardly focused, considerate, nurturing, encouraging, is emotional, and has many other feminine traits.

In our modern world, our roles have become confused. The emancipation of women has taken its toll and the patriarchal world has confused the divine masculine with power and force. Neither divine feminine nor divine masculine has to *force* its consciousness onto the world. It simply is.

Women have learned to allow their divine masculine to surface and dominate - and rightly so. We have had to invite our divine masculine into our outer world since we are required to hunt to feed our own future and to make masculine decisions. This has forced the divine masculine in men to feel emasculated and ineffective. And thus, our relationships no longer work.

How does the divine masculine coax the divine feminine out into the open? Is it even possible for the divine masculine to invite and encourage the divine feminine to come out into the world and to make her feel safe enough to emerge from her self-created cocoon of safety in order to surrender, without fear, to the divine masculine? Like men, women have been betrayed. They have been abandoned, beaten, used and abused and they have decided to take control of their own lives and learnt to provide what men used to provide. This journey has made them hard and unyielding, which is contrary to their true nature.

The divine feminine has gone into hiding because the divine masculine has forgotten that his primary task is to ensure that a woman walks safely upon the earth.

The divine masculine has, in turn, transformed itself into a vague image of what it should be. The masculine has used power and force to get what it desires. Because of this, the feminine has become imprisoned, and once the divine feminine tasted the freedom power and force brings, it neglects the true power of the feminine, which is nurturing and intuitive.

The divine masculine has gone into hiding because the divine feminine has forgotten that her primary task is to lead a man to his soul.

And neither get what they need to feel loved, honoured and respected. A woman needs to feel safe, protected and loved before she emerges from her prison of self-protection, and a man needs to feel respected and honoured before he will emerge from his prison of self-preservation.

When we no longer see the divine feminine as weak and submissive, and if we provide a safe space for the gentle side of the divine feminine within which to live, we may see the true divine feminine emerge once more. If we offer the divine masculine deep honour and respect, it may give up its need to be dominating and forceful and become the protector once more.

It is only when we surrender to the divine in each of us that we will find joy and love in our relationships once more

WE FORGET TO LOVE

18th August 2016

Today I woke up and saw myself again as I should. We forget, you see. We forget to love. We forget to be loving and we get caught up in our outer world, perpetuating the outer world's attitude. I have been teaching the merits of love for a long time now. Yet, I forget.

Today gives me an opportunity to choose again. Yesterday, a brave soul pointed out to me that I have become hypercritical. I rebelled against that immediately, and silently yelled, "You don't know me! You have no idea who I am." They clearly had no idea how fabulous I am or how long I have been teaching people to *choose love*. "Who does she think she is?" I thought silently and resentfully to myself.

I am extremely good at avoiding public snide remarks and I keep my arrogant, self-importance to myself. Yet, this morning, I woke up and decided to view myself truly. I decided that I would stay in the present moment and become aware of how often I am critical of anything or anyone.

It started with the kettle. I think it's about to break. Sometimes it doesn't switch on and I must wiggle the switch several times before it connects. That, in itself, is not the problem. The problem is my thoughts about the kettle and the hassle it would be to replace it, and wondering why things can't just be simple and easy for a change?

I took my coffee, opened the curtains and got back into bed. Immediately, the pillow was not right. I would have to replace the bloody pillow, and I was irritated about the garden. I wondered, "When is the rain coming?" Because it had not rained, I would have to go and water the garden again.

Then, God forbid, I opened my social media account. Almost every comment irritated me. I made a value judgment about everything: how wrong this one was and how bad that one's spelling and grammar was. How uninformed the next one was and how boring the other. How passive aggressive this one was. And God! Don't these people know how stupid they are? "Oh look," I thought, "Here is a really nice, uplifting post. Now *this* person is real! This one knows what true, loving behaviour is. I will *like* this post to show my support."

All this criticism occurred before 9 a.m. and I had not even left the house! I'm mortified. Between waking and writing this, a few hours have passed. And I hang my head in awareness – note awareness - not shame. "I'm sorry," I say to myself. "I'm sorry that I forgot that I could choose again. I choose love," and I sigh and try to become humble. I open my hardened heart - again.

"Forgive me, Father/Mother/Love, I know not what I do."

DEPRESSION AND ANXIETY

19th August 2016

Depression is yearning for the past. Anxiety is fear of the future. I know this sounds trite and I know only too well that once we are stuck in this spiral, it is very difficult to extricate oneself from this vortex. This spiral keeps us trapped in our pain. The longer we are trapped, the more this becomes a self-fulfilling prophecy.

Soon our family and friends become impatient with us. Not because they do not care, but because they do not know what to do to make us feel better. They certainly see and feel our pain and have compassion for it but feel helpless. This helplessness may cause them to begin to avoid us. There is no easy solution. There is only our own inner will and desire to survive that takes us from one day to the next. I know.

I'm slowly emerging from this cocoon of depression and anxiety. I know that the *only* thing that gets us out of this spiral is *action*.

If you are stuck in depression, write a plan for yourself and start with small tasks that you can manage. Don't let it be too challenging. For some of us, that may simply mean that you will have a shower. If that is all you can cope with today, then do that.

Isolation is a really big issue. It is easier to isolate ourselves than it is to face the world. This does not serve us at all. It furthers our belief that we need to bear this alone. And it's true, we have to bear this alone, it is our journey. Ultimately, we bear our journeys alone. Irrespective of what we tell ourselves when we are in this depressed and anxious state, that we aren't worthy of love. This is simply not true. Because we don't love ourselves, we project this non-love onto those who do love us. They do - they just feel helpless and do not know what we need in order for us to let go of our depression and anxiety. They can only stand by helplessly and watch us in our pain.

Only *action* will get us out of our self-imposed prison.

Get involved. Even when we don't feel like it, get out into the world. It helps if we can find something or someone where we can be of service. Being of service to others is often a catalyst, which will help to extricate us from our own prison of unworthiness. When we extend a hand to help others, even if we believe our own hand is broken, we slowly begin to feel worthy again.

Find something to which you can be of service and it will draw you out of your self-imposed hell.

FOR THOSE WHO ARE GRIEVING

31st August 2016

For those who have lost a loved one and for those who are watching them grieve, there is no time limit to grieving. Be aware that if someone you know has lost someone they love; time is what they need. Do not confuse time with moving on.

Just as you still speak about your ugly or sad divorce, which happened 20 years ago, so do those who are grieving speak of their own pain, or their departed loved one as well. Don't expect them to move on. They are simply expressing their pain or memories, just as you are. This loss is a significant experience in their lives.

Please remember, there are triggers that ignite their sadness. These triggers can be a birthday, Christmas, New Year or the anniversary of their loved one's death - all significant events for those who have lost someone. People who are grieving don't need pity, they need understanding. Special or significant days are supposed to be shared with those we love, and if we have lost a loved one, those days will forever have a wistful sadness to them, even though those who grieve seemed to have moved on.

Those who have lost a loved one will always need to talk about them. Let them. Just as you talk about a happy experience when you holidayed in France five years ago, so will they remember the good times they spent with their departed loved one.

Sometimes, those who have not lost a loved one expect the recall of memories of the deceased spouse or family member to stop. Why? Those memories are just as valid for the one who lost a loved one than for those whose loved ones are still alive. They are reminiscing – and that is okay. That does not mean they are not moving on. It simply means they remember with fondness, just like you, and may feel like sharing a memory.

If you are uncomfortable when those who have lost a loved one speak about the dead, be sure to inspect your own discomfort about death and dying. When those who speak about the good times they shared with their loved ones, the audience often seems uncomfortable. Examine this discomfort in yourself. If you were speaking about a memory you had when you were skiing in the Alps with your wife, nobody becomes uncomfortable.

We don't speak about our lost loved ones because we have not moved on. We speak about them because they were a part of our lives and we wish to celebrate those memories. If you go quiet on us or avoid speaking about the dead, we feel you don't care and that you wish for us to remove all memory of our departed loved one. We have moved on, we just sometimes remember the pain or the joy, just as we remember and share the painful and joyful events in our life.

There may be the odd tear - even years later. That is as it should be. If the odd tear does not happen, it would mean that we did not feel love. It's just the same as a memory we may have that is just so precious that it brings a tear to our eye. Perhaps a memory of when our child was very ill, or a tear of joy when our partner recovered after a car accident. Those tears are normal.

They may be the tears of our memories about the intense fear we felt and then the relief that goes with the discovery that all will be well.

Those tears happen because we cared, not because we have not moved on. And they will happen, especially when it is a birthday or the anniversary of a death. Just as we celebrate our child's birthday, and memories of the actual day of their birth flood our minds, so do memories of our dead loved ones flood our minds on those days. Yet, we have moved on. We are just remembering in this moment. If you tell us not to cry, we feel isolated in our memories. We cry - just as you do, over happy and sad memories.

Telling someone who is grieving how *lucky* they were to have had the love and joy and how *lucky* they were to have had so many years with a departed loved one, and telling them *that they are still with us,* is not helpful. They miss their loved one's physical touch, the sound of their voice and their smell. They will never hear their voices again and they will never feel their touch again. Just allow them to feel the loss without telling them how *lucky* they are, or that they will forever be with them.

Just let us grieve when we need to. Their physical bodies are gone. We will never see them again. We have our own view of the spiritual side. This would be as hurtful as telling someone how *lucky* they just lost a leg when they could have died. Tragedy is never lucky.

When the time is right, we will move on. Moving on does not mean our loved one never existed and that we will never speak of them again. We speak of them because we remember and because we loved them - just as you do.

There is no yin without yang, there is no joy without pain, there is no laughter without tears, there is no up if there is no down. There is no light if there is no darkness. It's about finding balance and acknowledging *both* sides of who we are. Denying one part of us has never, and will never, serve us. When we deny someone's pain, we deny their love and joy as well.

THE BANE OF UNSOLICITED ADVICE

7th September 2016

How often do we open our mouths and presume to offer *unsolicited* advice?

A friend and I were in my kitchen preparing salads for lunch. She was making a mixed, green salad and I was peeling potatoes. I noticed that she was becoming more and more agitated. Soon she took a potato out of my hand and said, "If you peel them like this, it goes much quicker." I have been peeling potatoes for more than 40 years!

I have observed many women and men give advice when their partners are doing something. When your man makes your bed, do you tell him how it should be done? How often do you tell your wife how to drive?

It seems if we make a statement to our friends, there will be those few who will always offer advice, even before we have had the opportunity to finish our story and had time to relate how we resolved the situation. The same person will consistently offer unsolicited advice, tell you how to do it, or what to do.

We offer constant, and often unsolicited, advice on how to be pregnant, raise children, drive cars, conduct ourselves at the doctor's office, write a letter, open a can of beans, hang washing on the line, eat healthy food, make investments, why someone should stop smoking, make peace with a friend, serve tea, mow the lawn, get a job, how to be more at peace, quit boxing, deal with your child's teacher, overcome obstacles, deal with pain, how to deal with grief, hang curtains and just about anything else one can imagine.

We say things such as, if you just spend more time in medita-tion, focus more on your self-confidence, be kinder, take cannabis oil, stop drinking/taking drugs, watch less TV, eat organic food, take fewer pills, invite God/spirit into your life, focus more on the positive, let go of the past, then you will be happier, enlightened, or go to heaven.

There are those who simply cannot help themselves and always have a better, quicker, more effective way to do, and deal with, just about anything. Their way is the right way, often accompa-nied by, "I'm just trying to help." God forbid you offer *them* advice. They are instantly offended because they already know the perfect way to do just about anything.

I am not suggesting that this is done maliciously. Often, it is not. I think we have just fallen into the habit of giving unsolicited advice. I know how much it irritates me - and I know I do it as well. I try to remind myself, "Unless you hear the words, *please help me*, shut up."

This is harder than one thinks. Sometimes, when I catch myself offering someone unsolicited advice, and this only really happens when I am conscious, I may even apologise and say something like, "OMG, I'm telling you how to do this." or "There I go again, telling you what to do."

It is difficult to break the habit of giving unsolicited advice. Assume you are dealing with an adult, and that they have their *own* way of doing things. If you are unclear whether you should offer advice ask, "Are you just venting, or do you want my advice or help?"

Do not offer advice at all, if you have not actually experienced what the individual is going through, because you have no idea. Simply support them to process the situation in whatever way they feel they need. Do not presume to know how a person is feeling if you have not experienced the same thing.

Unsolicited advice is just that – unsolicited – and it is often unwelcome.

Unless you hear the words, "Please help me," just empathise without offering advice by reflecting their feelings back to them. We know this and yet we fail to apply it. We all have our own way of dealing with and doing things.

AN INNER JOURNEY

11th September 2016

Spirituality is not about how many Guru quotes or bible verses you know. It is not about raising your vibration. It is not about telling others how much you love God, Jesus or Shiva. It is not about daily meditation. It is not about letting go. It is not about creating sacred space. It is not about mantras. It is not about typing amen. It is not about chanting. It is not about clearing your energy. It is not about anything *out there* or anything external to yourself.

It is about being nice. Just be nice. Just be nicer today than you were yesterday. Just be nice - even to the people who are drunk or stoned at traffic lights. Be nice to your neighbours and be nice to the policeman. Be nice to people who do not believe as you believe, and don't forget to be nice to yourself, because if you are nice to yourself, you'll be inclined to be nicer to others. Be nice!

Please feel free to replace the word nice with loving, kind, generous, fun, accepting and other cool words like that.

ALLOWING GRIEF

22nd September 2016

Please let people be sad. Please allow people to mourn. We are not allowed to mourn but we *should* mourn. It is not just death we should mourn. We really should allow ourselves to mourn the loss of a marriage. We don't do that. People expect us to leave the courtroom with a smile on our faces and join our friends at our divorce celebration. But below any relief we may feel at finally being divorced, we should mourn the loss of our dream. When we first married, we dreamed that it would last forever. It is that dream that we should mourn, the death of that dream.

There are many other occasions that we realistically should allow ourselves to mourn. Take time to mourn. I am not suggesting that we should throw ourselves on the floor in the middle of a shopping centre and cry uncontrollably. I'm suggesting that we should be kinder to ourselves. And just because society doesn't allow us to mourn, it doesn't mean that we should deny ourselves the healing effect of mourning a loss – any loss.

WHAT IS SPIRITUALITY?

22nd November 2016

Spirituality does not depend on how often you meditate, or how many crystals you have. It is not about your healing ability or your arcane knowledge. It is not about how many books you have read, or the Masters you channel. It is not about how many workshops and seminars you have attended.

It is about peace in your heart. It is about the love you are able to show. It is about the compassion you have for the circumstances of others. It is about the generosity of your heart.

The only thing you truly have to share with the world is that which resides in your heart. Let there be lightness in your heart. Let there be joy and most of all, let there be love.

THE BLAME GAME

19th January 2017

Has the New Age or spiritual movement embarked on a massive blame-game exercise? Has this blame game snuck in without us being conscious of it and is it detrimental to our humanity? I think so.

The more I see statements such as "Being positive gets you the best life." And, "Focusing on the now and letting go of the past is the way to success and freedom," the more I feel that I am somehow not doing enough, not meditating enough, not being positive enough and not focusing on my goals enough, and that this is the reason why things are not working as well for me as they should.

Have we recreated the old and traditional dogma of heaven and hell? Am I now not achieving my goals, because I am not living my life as positively as I can? Is my current *downward trend* happening because I am doing something wrong? Is it like a *punishment* of sorts because of my lack of meditation or positivity?

Believe me that I, of all people, have been down this road of saying and believing these things. I have a dream board, I focus on being positive, I take appropriate action. In fact, how many people have I assisted in achieving their goals?

The longer I am on my journey towards *enlightenment*, the more I realise that there is no enlightenment.

There is only love and compassion, huge amounts of compassion. There is only letting go of judgement. There is only kindness. There is only service. It never was about anything else. It was never about the crystals, or meditation, or even the prayer and the belief in any sort of afterlife. These things are only valuable if they are leading us toward love. It is about love. It has only ever been about love.

It is about understanding and having compassion for the situation of another without telling them that if they are just a little more positive, good things will happen. It is about helping others. It is about opening actual doors, like an introduction to your human resources department, or buying someone some needed groceries, or filling someone's tank with fuel, or volunteering at the local orphanage or animal shelter, or washing someone's hair, or running someone a bath. It is about *doing* something for someone else.

And sometimes, it's simply about giving someone a hug and telling them how much they mean to us. It isn't, and never has been, about preaching the *word*, whether that word was from your preferred holy book, or from *The Secret*. When you are distressed about something, imagine being asked, "So what did you *do* to attract this situation into your life?"

We never know where someone is at right now in their lives. We never know the depth of someone else's despair. We never know the depth of someone else's loneliness. And if we offer them a lecture about being positive, this may very well just make them feel more inadequate. Perhaps they are just exhausted.

Life sometimes throws us incredibly curved balls that we could never have anticipated. Telling someone that they must pray, or believe, or meditate more, or be more positive is not constructive. They probably know this and are probably doing those things.

Oh, how I wish I can be in this space of understanding all the time. How I wish I can practise unconditional love. Oh, how I wish I can live with empathy all the time. Forgive me for the times that I have offered you a lecture instead of offering you love, help and compassion.

Please, forgive me.

THAT IN-BETWEEN SPACE

13th Feb 2017

There is an in-between space in which some souls find themselves - too sick or unsure to go and too sick or unsure to stay. It is the in-between space where they are not strong enough to choose. Perhaps they do not even know that choice is an option.

That in-between space that is hell for the observers is perhaps a darker hell for the soul who is there.

Yet, I am not sure if the soul knows that it is in-between. Sometimes, chemicals course through the veins, machines chime, beep and tic, and we are in this in-between space. How can we be sure the soul of the sick person is even in the room? We know that the soul is still tethered, or else the heart would cease beating. How do we know the in-between soul's desire? How do we know? How do we know? Do we switch everything off? Do we do more harm in the hope that this last attempt to save a life will bring us to a turning point? Will the next effort be the turning point that will see the light return to the body's eyes? And even then, do we really know that the journey forward is the journey this soul chooses?

When a soul we love is in that in-between space, now that - that is special kind of hell!

ABOUT GRIEF

18th February 2017

I know this road. I have been on it before. It is a long road and a road we can only take alone. There are people along this road. And they are the ones who encourage us to take the next step. Or encourage us to take time out to sit under a tree and contemplate the journey. But we travel the road itself alone. Yet, without those along the roadside, the journey would seem so much harder.

When we lose someone we love, it is an inner journey we travel. The ripples of the loss touch many people. Those who loved the departed travel on their own version of this road. Those who support us are also on this road or alongside it: waiting and watching.

Some do not know how to support the bereaved and are too afraid to ask us what we need, so they stay away. They stay away not because they don't care. They stay away because they don't know how to bear our pain. Some fly in with their support and want our pain to leave us. They mean well, but our pain is our pain and the road we are on is the road. Others tell us that our beloved is in a better place or they remind us that our beloved is still with us. This does not console us. We know this and we get it. But it does nothing for our pain.

There are those who tell us how they think we should handle this road. How we should grieve, or what we should try to ease our pain. Their way is their way and ours is ours. We cannot do it their way, for this is our road.

There are those who are able to sit with us, and just be there. They do not wish the pain to be anything other than what it is. They do not do anything other than allow us our sadness. This is mostly what we need. Perhaps we need food.

Sometimes this pain of loss makes us thrash around. Afrikaans is a very expressive language and it is best described as, "*Dit is 'n geween en 'n gekners van tande.*" Yes, sometimes it is that. Other times our mourning takes us into a quiet, inward journey and from the outside it may look as though we are gone - gone to a far-away place where nobody can follow. It is that as well. Other times, silent tears simply roll down our cheeks.

Sometimes we stare at a photo, or hold onto an item of clothing, or hear a piece of music, or hear a child's laughter, or a word, or a look, or a phrase, and these flood our memories. Eventually, these memories will no longer make us cry. Eventually. Until then, allow those memories to do to us as they will without trying to make it better. It isn't better. Not yet.

Above all else, it is the loss of love that we mourn. The love we held for the individual who has passed. They showed their love for us in so many ways. We all remember the departed because of the love they showed us, however that manifested.

Now, we no longer have it. We miss it and yearn for it. It is hard to be without that love. We know that others love us as well. We know and we appreciate it. But today, today we are mourning the love of the departed because we know we will never again hear their voice, feel their touch, or hear their laughter.

THE LOVE AND FEAR DICHOTOMY

6th April 2017

I have yet to meet a person who can love what is so, all the time. We are the human race. We are hard-wired for the love/fear dichotomy. If any human being is capable of loving what is so in every minute of every day, I'd love to meet them.

A situation, such as our current political one, is a case in point. We love what is in alignment with our own conscious evolution. We disapprove of its opposite.

Yet, it is still the eternal yin and yang. All we can really say is that something does not serve us, and if many of us feel that something does not serve us any longer, we can get together to change it. Yet, if we change it with anger and hatred, we tend to become that anger and hatred. History has shown us time and time again that victims become perpetrators. It is therefore very difficult to be in this world but not of it.

The ANC and others changed the situation when they rose up en masse to change a regime that did not serve them. Their regime, in turn, will eventually also fall. It is like that all over the world. Countries that were once strong and vibrant are no longer that. Countries that were once insignificant are now rising to their full potential.

I am not suggesting that I am not uncomfortable about the political situation: I am. I wish to rant and rave and be outraged. I have to keep asking myself, "What would love do and whom does it serve." Will it make a difference? What will it do to me and my body if I should succumb to ranting and raving? Will it still be uncomfortable and disillusioned after the ranting? Will it change the way I feel about the situation?

Then I ask myself, "What can I do about the current situation?" Nothing! All I can do is try to hold love in my heart. I can feel love for our beautiful country, love for its people, and I can try to be understanding of its diversity.

Where one has diversity, one often has conflict, because the human race is not evolved enough to love what is not like them. Fear still governs our anatomy, our very consciousness. Primitive flight or fight chemicals govern our bodies. The human race is simply built that way. The best I can do in our current political situation is attempt to stay in a space of love.

I will try and do that and I will attempt to minimise my own judgement, disapproval and hatred.

EVERYTHING IS ENERGY

11 April 2017

We know that everything is energy, right? We do. Yes? Science has shown us that. We also know that hatred begets hatred and that love begets love. Right? I also know that there are people who thrive on the pain of others and that there are people who thrive on the love and joy in the lives of others. This has been so since the beginning of time.

We also know that on whatever we focus our attention, we receive more of in our lives. Right? We know this. We also know that 'tit for tat' behaviour does not work. We also know that telling someone else they are wrong, and we are right, does nothing for peace? Furthermore, history has shown us that victims become perpetrators. It takes a really evolved being not to become a perpetrator.

I'm calling on aware and awake people who know all of the above. I'm calling on them to step up and truly be the wisdom seekers and peacemakers. I'm calling on the awake and aware people to cease participation in this demeaning struggle for right and wrong in South Africa and the world. I'm calling on you to be the peacemakers and the way-finders. Find a way to be respectful of all others.

I am asking those who want to find another way to talk about this other way. I'm asking you not to celebrate the destructive behaviour of others by sharing it on social media and giving it any of our energy. Rather, find that which is uplifting and inspiring about our beautiful world and share that.

We give our time to those who are belligerent and disrespectful and in this way, we create more drama and discontent around a situation, which feeds more fears and creates more chaos and hatred.

I call on those who are the wisdom seekers, the peaceful ones, the ones who have honour and respect, I call on you not to give up who you are. You are the wisdom seekers! Another's behaviour and actions should not be able to change who you are.

Be the wisdom seeker. Be the peacemaker. Be the beacon of light, irrespective of the behaviour and actions of others.

It is the wisdom seekers and the peacemakers who will find another way.

A SIMPLER LIFE

21st April 2017

"What is wrong? You don't sound okay," you asked. I immediately replied, "No, don't worry, I'm okay." We all do this. All the time. This question was asked of me by someone who knows me really well.

We live in such isolation from each other. Some of us are embarrassed that we do not seem to be coping with life, especially those of us who seem outwardly so strong, and especially those of us who know that our thinking creates our experience of reality. Therefore, if we could only change our thinking, then our reality, surely, must change.

What if we can't? What if we are just stuck? What if we are just bone weary?

I do believe in the journey of the soul. I do believe that we reincarnate and that in each lifetime we learn new lessons. What if...? What if in *this* lifetime, we simply bit off more than we could chew? What if we are teachers and have taught so many others how to be positive, how to grow as a person and yet, here we are, stuck.

So many of my *old soul* friends seem to be battling - those who are the peaceful ones and the storytellers. We seem to be battling the same dragon, even if our dragon is on a different plane. The issues with which we are battling seem to be different. Some of us are battling with broken marriages. Some of us battle with the wars waging in the corporate or business world. Some of us are battling with the death of loved ones. Others are battling with the scars of a dysfunctional childhood. Most of us are battling with the state of the world - not just the environment but the cruelty to our animals, and the state of constant war. Many of us battle with constant violence and relentless race issues.

I am tired and many of my gentle friends are tired. We hold open our hearts and we hold sacred space for others. We teach as we learn, and we inspire and encourage as we grow. Perhaps this is an existential crisis. Perhaps we have just done enough *growing* in this lifetime. Perhaps we choose not to *learn* any more lessons and perhaps we just want to find a tree next to a river and sit under it and stare at the water. Perhaps we just want to sit with our feet in the soothing stream and shut the world out. We want to forget about death and war and hatred and meanness and anger and rage. We want to forget about race wars and murder and missiles. We want to let go of sickness and death, prisons, and fear.

I know that the opposite exists. I know about flowers and joy and abundance. I know about those. I remember. I'm normally the one reminding others about that.

Like so many of my friends who are healers and storytellers, I am bone weary. I yearn for my village where children play in the sand and elders sit in the sun. I yearn for the singing and the fires and the hunting and the gathering. I yearn for co-operation and sharing. I yearn for the disagreements and medicine women, and I yearn for the wise ones who helped us come to peace about our disagreements. I yearn for the simple life.

We thought we were so clever, building big machines and mega-factories that were supposed to make our lives easier. All that did was make the walls higher and teach us that there was not enough.

Come with me to a faraway land where fairies roam and dragons fly. Come fly with me to a place where we can build reed boats and laugh when we fall into the water. Come with me to where life is about sunrise and sunset and rhythm and peace, where I can teach you to make a basket and you can show me the value of your story.

A PRAYER

22nd April 2017

Since it's time, and a day of prayer in South Africa, I wish to offer one as well.

Dear (put the name of the being you believe to be sacred here, even if it is your own soul or heart)

I ask that you give me the strength to keep my temper in check. Guide me to speak only that which is inspiring and uplifting. Please show me how to keep hatred out of my heart and learn tolerance, even if others are not tolerant.

Please help me to find enough compassion to assist those in need. Please (Sacred being's name), allow me to let others grow at their own pace and give me the courage to show others, by my example, how to make the world a better place.

I ask for leniency and understanding for all the times that I have hurt others, and the times I have been disrespectful. I ask for understanding for the times that I have tried to change others by means of violence, pressure, manipulation, domination, or force.

I ask for tolerance and understanding for the times that I have behaved in a superior way. I ask for understanding and compassion for the times that I have made others wrong because they don't live where I live, believe what I believe, own what I own, or speak the language that I do.

I ask (Sacred being's name), that I find the wisdom to explore a way towards tolerance, compassion, kindness and love in everything I do.

I know that if I am all of these things, I will contribute to making the world a better place.

This is what I wish for most of all: for the world to be a kinder, more peaceful and gentler place, filled with love rather than fear and hatred. I know that in order to achieve that I have to *be* that. I ask this in thy/my name.

And so it is.

Amen

WANT BETTER RELATIONSHIPS?

1st May 2017

1) Be kind

Always. Just be kind. Unkind words can never be unsaid. We can never reverse unkind deeds. And even if you have been forgiven for your unkindness, the wounds don't go away and will still be there 30 years later.

2) Keep things in perspective

This one thing that has upset you is not an indication of your whole relationship. It is one thing. There are 999 other things that are good right in this moment. Don't let one thing or event destroy your relationship.

3) Say what you need

If you do not say what you need, how do you expect to get your heart's desire? Make it clear. If you need space right now, make sure the people around you know that and tell them why. Make sure they know that even though you need space, you still love them.

4) Own your own crap

Everyone carries around past pain. Do not blame others for the crap that went on in your past. If the memory still hurts you, and if you lash out at a partner or friend because they touched a raw memory nerve, know it's your crap that is setting you off, not their intention to upset you.

5) Allow others their feelings

If the other person is angry or upset, don't try to make their feelings not okay by negating them. If someone is angry or sad, allow them to have their feelings, even if you have set them off. Love them through their feelings and discuss them when both parties are calm and open.

These five things are a great start to better relationships.

6) Don't be so offended

Being offended by how people dress, what they believe, who they date, how they paint their nails, or their sexual preference is exhausting. Let that shit go.

7) Give up your need to be right

These pointless arguments about who is right and who is wrong are so meaningless. There is simply no ultimate truth. There is only our perspective of it. Do you want to be right or do you want it to work?

8) Mind your own business

We are so quick to get on the bandwagon and talk about other people's business. There are three kinds of business: Your Business, Other people's Business and God's business. Ask yourself often, "Whose business am I in?"

9) Stop fuelling the fires of anger/outrage

Some people simply love adding fuel to the fire and inciting people to more anger and outrage. If you cannot stay at peace with yourself, your loved ones, or your neighbours, at least do not incite others to participate in your rage. And 'tit for tat' behaviour has never ever solved an issue.

10) Stop interfering or offering advice

Incessantly *suggesting* to others how they must feel, behave, do something, react, and giving an endless stream of advice is tiresome. Unless you hear the words, "Please help me," shut up. Offering unsolicited advice just sucks - stop it! If you are unclear about this ask, "Are you just venting or are you asking for advice?"

WHY I QUIT MY SPIRITUAL JOURNEY

10th May 2017

I've given up my *spiritual path* in favour of the human path. I gave it up some time ago and I'm much better off for it. The spiritual path requires that I give up my ego.

Yet, my ego is the part of me that is attached to what's right and what's wrong - that eternal dichotomy of life on earth: good versus evil, pain and pleasure, darkness and light.

Soul, or spirit, on the other hand, is unattached and egoless and detached from our lives on earth. It holds no value judgement about pain or pleasure, happiness or sadness, joy or compassion. Soul or spirit only sees that which is so - without judgment. An egoless state accepts that what is so, is so.

The soul or spirit has no need of learning or knowledge because it is already all learning and all knowledge. It knows it is part of God-consciousness and as such it has nothing to learn, to do, or to be - it just is. It is that which is all-potential and no-potential all at the same time. It is the unconditional space of acceptance of what is so without making anything right or wrong. That's what unconditional means - accepting what is so unconditionally.

Ego, from my perspective, is that part of me residing in the core of who I am. That part that makes me feel uncomfortable when I am unkind or mean, or niggles at me when I am talking behind someone's back. Yet, it is also that part of me that weeps at the sight of a sunset and feels elated when a friend achieves greatness. It is that part of me that makes me uniquely human and humane - or not.

My ego is that part of me that awakens a desire to be better, to reach higher. It is also that part of me that hates and rages. And in that, I have a choice. As we all do. We all have an internal barometer that tells us if our actions are *good or bad*. And we all know when we are not living our highest truth. We all know this because our internal barometer tells us.

I'm off the *spiritual path* and I am now a seeker of joy. I am a seeker of human laughter and compassion and nurturing and giving. I have spent many years seeking enlightenment and I have found only ego. I have only found the same, tired ideas cloaked in new words, where heaven and hell are replaced by ascension and karma, where warnings of hell have a different face. This new face says, "You are to blame because you are not mindful enough. You don't meditate enough. You have poverty consciousness." Is that not just another hell?

I will seek the ego path and its eternal choice of right and wrong, seeking to stay on the right side, the side that makes me glad from the inside. And as with all things, I will be on this particular merry-go-round for a while and then probably decide I should do some soul searching once more.

That is the life of the seeker. As soon as we find something, we change direction.

May your path be straight and easy and your learning quick and painless.

FOCUS ON THE POSITIVE

22nd May 2017

Many years ago, after doing public speaking for a while, it dawned on me that after every talk some people would come up to me and tell me how wonderful my talk was.

Sometimes, there would be one who would come up and tell me that I was talking nonsense or they disliked or disagreed with it. For days and days afterwards, I'd hang onto those negative comments and worry about my next talk. Could I do better? Perhaps I should do more research. I could present it in a friendlier way. The negative comment had filled me with self-doubt and rebukes.

One day, I realised that I was giving my power to those who did not like my work and disregarded all those who did. I made an immediate switch and decided that I would focus my gratitude on those who love my work and simply let go of those who did not.

It was a hard lesson.

WE ARE THE CHOSEN ONES

22nd May 2017

"We are the chosen ones" is an opening line on a Christian church's social media post. I find this to be so arrogant.

God: It does not matter to me what you call that which you consider divine intelligence or even whether you believe in anything divine. How arrogant it is to assume we can even name it? For me, God is unfathomable.

In *one* of our holy books, it says, "There is nowhere that I am not." Just this one statement makes all the wars, the disagreements, and the terror that has been bestowed on the world in the name of God, obsolete.

I also find the fact that someone believes their way of serving God is the one and only true way to be bizarre. They should, therefore, take responsibility for their part in the hatred caused by this belief that their way is the right way - hatred caused in the name of their God.

Bearing in mind that the other holy books also say that their way is the only true way, it is unthinkable when that same holy book also says that God is love. There simply cannot be hatred - of any sort - if God is love. It doesn't matter how we serve God, or how we choose to pray, or which name we choose to use. I feel the same way about the *spiritual* believers, who have simply made *their* way the right way.

If, "There is nowhere that I am not," is an accepted *truth*, surely people understand that God is also in the Imam and the Rabbi and the Sufi. If we really sit back and think about it, if God is eternal and everywhere, that alone should be unfathomable.

This means that this divine force is in the drug dealer, the child molester, the church, the mosque, the mother and the child, the tree and the sand, the joint and the medicine, and in every star in the universe. We cannot even fathom the universe let alone comprehend God.

This makes the idea that on a tiny little planet called Earth, on the backside of our small, insignificant solar system, people are waging wars about whose God is the right and true God.

I like to think of God as that which makes the atoms and/or molecules move. If that were true, the statement, "There is nowhere that I am not," makes sense to me. This way of seeing God brings me to a point where I am no longer able to assign human characteristics to divinity.

It is far too great a force to assign mere human characteristics to something so vast that I cannot even get my little, human brain to fathom it, let alone to prescribe to others how they must view, serve, praise or understand God.

For me, the ultimate blasphemy is killing in the name of God. I am saddened by humanity's need to make wrong how others serve the divine. I find it arrogant beyond measure that they even think that they are chosen by God. How can they be chosen? Every atom in their body is part of the divine that some call God. "There is nowhere that I am not." This is like saying that your pinkie nail chooses you.

ENCOURAGED TO HATE

24th May 2017

Those in power perpetuate this hatred between white and black, or Christian and Muslim.

While we spend our time squabbling with each other and feeding our hatred frenzy, those in power laugh. I'm not saying that the hatred is not real - it is - and that is really the sad part. We are literally killing each other over it.

The hatred comes about because those in power want it to be there. You see, if Christians did not fear or hate Muslims, we would not support our governments in the creation of war. It is not war, per se, that the governments want, it is the continued success of large corporations.

These large corporations control resources such as oil and gold and the huge arms industry. And *this* is where the 1% get to stay the 1%.

Because we continue to be given reasons to hate someone who is not like us, the powers that be can be sure that their continued war will be supported, and they can continue to manufacture the weapons that destroy our peace.

They supply these weapons to *both* sides. And we let them

because we perpetuate the hate. Race hatred is no different. While we, at grassroots level, continue to hate each other because of the colour of our skin, the powers that be will continue to feed that hatred on their public platforms because they know, whilst we are scrabbling in the dirt worrying about who said what racial slurs to whom, they can raid and pillage our beloved country.

Why? Well, because they feel fully justified to steal from one race group, while in reality, they are stealing from *all* of the people in South Africa, not just one race group.

While we can sit in our little ivory tower of hate and disapproval, the people on the other side of the race wars can say, "You see? They deserve to have their possessions taken by force." They may even justify that the lives of some may indiscriminately be taken, because of an unjust past. Then the indignant side can say, "You see? They are unable to be reasonable or fair. They truly are savages." And we continue to hate while the rape and pillage of our country continues. Neither side sees the truth because we are too busy perpetuating the hate.

Just when we begin to settle down and begin to believe that everything is going to be okay, an often-manufactured *event* occurs that stirs up the hate once more - just to keep the masses in line. This event ensures that we perpetuate the hate once more. The 1% here in South Africa is no different from the 1% anywhere else in the world. Hatred is perpetuated because those in power know that it works to distract the majority of the population and the status quo remains intact.

FEAR IS REAL

29th May 2017

Fear is debilitating. Fear can paralyse. Yet, I understand that fear is a chemical reaction in my body. Fear causes stress in the body, which releases hormones and chemicals to try to rectify the balance to prepare my body for flight or fight and freeze or fold.

We know that stress can cause illness. Therefore, pretending that fear caused by stress or any other reason is not real, doesn't help the average person. All it does is cause us to feel that we are somehow doing something wrong because we feel fearful. This just makes us feel that it is our fault that we are sick. If you are feeling fearful, you are feeling fearful. Denying what you feel is counterproductive.

I believe that the better way to deal with this is to teach any individual that we can *manage* fear. We know when our bodies are out of control due to fear. We fret and stress and if it is severe, there may be physical symptoms, such as rapid heartbeat, sweaty palms and a great deal more. Fear can even cause depression. A slow heart rate with stress chemical release can cause feelings of hopelessness or helplessness.

We can bring our body chemistry back under control and once we do this, the fear will subside. We can do this by focusing all our energy on our heart – the heart being the centre of our universe. Focus on the heart for about two minutes, then imagine that you can breathe through your heart, breathing deeply and evenly for about two minutes. Continue to breathe and then change this focus and inhale and exhale the feeling of peace and harmony for a further two minutes. While we do this, the body will automatically stop producing stress chemicals and begin to release feel-good chemicals.

The more we learn to deal with our body's state of fear, the more we can control our behaviour so that we do not react from a place of fear. The trick is, of course, to *know* when we are at the mercy of our own internal stress chemistry. Prolonged exposure to stress hormones can and does cause illness.

Manage the body's chemistry and manage the fear. Pretending that fear does not exist or isn't real, does not serve anyone. Positive thinking is not going to change the fact that your body is releasing fear and stress chemicals. It is. Learn how to manage it so that we can minimise the intensity of our fear.

MAINTAINING PEACE

10th June 2017

How do we stay peaceful amid all the race-baiting that is going on? How do we stay at peace with the mindless killing? How do we remain peaceful amid the race rage issue even though we are outraged at the mindlessness of the violence?

People from all cultures and all religions are bone weary. We are bone weary at the disrespect and dishonour. We are all outraged that there are people in our social circle who are racist, sexist, ageist and just plain bad, or unconscious. People of all races and cultures can do bad things and will continue to do them.

I know from bitter experience that telling someone they are wrong has the opposite effect of what I am trying to achieve. I know from self-experience that if someone tells me that I should not feel what I feel, that I get hugely resentful and rebellious. I also know from bitter experience that anger ignites anger and hatred begets more hatred.

Does it work if we post our outrage on social media? I don't think so.

I'm not suggesting that we bury our heads in the sand either.

What is going on isn't okay. How we have been dealing with it doesn't work!

We know apartheid did not work. We know that. We know that fighting does not work. We also know that ignoring it does not work.

I don't profess to have the answers. I'm asking that everyone become more aware. Become more aware of the times that race-baiting articles are published on social media. Become aware that we get hooked into the outrageousness of the article and we lash out in response.

More often than not, these articles come from fake news sites and are specifically designed to get a negative reaction. If we share these articles, we are just helping to fuel the race fires and that serves no-one, least of all the person who is sharing the articles. I'm asking everyone to become more mindful. Ask yourself, before you share your outrage on social media, just take a minute and ask yourself, "Am I making the situation worse, or am I making the situation better?"

I'm hoping that I can be conscious enough to just take a moment to err on the side of sanity. I am hoping that I can get to a place where I would rather say, "Forgive them, Father, for they know not what they do." If I can only stay at that level of consciousness.

INDESTRUCTIBLE SOUL

11th June 2017

Nothing can tarnish, destroy, impress, violate, or damage your soul. You can't sell it to the devil. It can't be hurt, disappointed, shocked, or surprised. It simply is!

It has no ego and therefore cannot judge. It can only experience what is so in total acceptance or Agapé.

Your soul has always been and will always be.

BELIEF SYSTEMS

13th June 2017

Creating a belief system, irrespective of how altruistic you believe the belief system to be, is still just that: a belief system.

Many spiritual believers are of the opinion that if we could change or raise our vibrational frequency, we would be able to time travel, or be in two places at a time or manifest material things out of mid-air. In my view, we are here to attain mastery. Masters will simply be able to do these things effortlessly – without thought or belief. Michael says, "Belief is not required. A leaf does not have to believe in photosynthesis to turn green."

An example of a belief system could be the firm belief some may have that if our children play outside in the cold and wet weather, they will get sick. Even though we logically know that a virus makes our children sick, not the weather.

Many have also created a belief system that being vegetarian is the only way to achieve enlightenment. Please be sure that I am not suggesting that the way we treat animals is acceptable. How we treat animals is a different discussion to the belief that one cannot achieve enlightenment unless one is vegetarian.

Any belief system that we can create on this planet contributes perfectly to the purpose of this planet, which is in its very essence – duality; yin and yang, good and evil, high and low, hot or cold. In a system that is driven by duality, absolutely anything that we create on this planet will contribute to the system of duality.

My purpose on this planet is to accept that this is a planet of duality. I firmly believe that those who are working towards finishing their cycle on this planet will cease to find any belief system at all – given that even that is a belief system. When we are ready to cycle off to a more enlightened planet, we will no longer participate in the creation of belief systems that support duality. I believe that those who are near the end of their cycle of lives on this planet will achieve mastery. To achieve mastery of what is so and loving what is so, is, for me, the ultimate goal.

Therefore, whether we are vegetarian, smoke, don't smoke, take vitamins, eat healthily, only eat organic or are on a light-only diet is completely irrelevant. The belief we have around these things is quite telling and will determine whether we achieve mastery or not.

Whilst we may vehemently believe in the acceptability of one way, for instance, vegetarianism, it will not necessarily raise our vibrational frequency or effect any lasting change on this planet for as long as we believe our way is the right way. Whilst we proselytise that our way is right and the way of others is wrong, we are still playing into the delicious yin and yang of the planet. This is not mastery.

For me, mastery is accepting what is so. That means honouring the path of everyone: vegetarians and non-vegetarians, believers and atheists, healthy eaters and unhealthy eaters, peaceful ones and violent ones. This is our dearest planet of duality. It can be no different; it is the planet where we learn about duality. Earth is the master class in duality. When we can get to a place of just loving what is so, we will achieve mastery.

When we are ready to *graduate* from this planet, we will surrender to its very nature and love its duality. We will no longer make one side of the same coin right and the other wrong. This is the hardest thing for me to do. Loving what is so instead of trying to change people and preaching my truth. And then I do just that – preach.

LOVE, WISDOM AND POWER

16th June 2017

LOVE: If you love, love with everything you have. I have heard many an abused woman say, "I stay because he is a good father." This means you are powerless in the relationship and lack the wisdom to see the truth. Therefore, love without power and wisdom can make you a doormat.

WISDOM: Wisdom that is not shared is meaningless. Therefore, wisdom without the power (means) to share it, or the love (desire) to share it makes it only knowledge. Share your wisdom.

POWER: Power without wisdom and love is seldom a great thing. Power without those two can and does corrupt. If you are in a position of power, may you have enough wisdom and love to use it wisely.

The combination of love, wisdom and power gives me the courage and the strength to face the challenges of life and it opens my heart to compassion and caring without making me feel small or diminished.

As we know, the power of the Trinity is universal. I can even relate this concept to a Christian tradition: God is Power. Holy

Spirit is Wisdom. Jesus is Love. When I am in my highest state of consciousness, I am in a state of Agapé. My own personal Holy Trinity.

DON'T BEAT YOURSELF UP

16th June 2107

Don't beat yourself up because you lost your temper for a minute. Sometimes letting off steam is equal to years of therapy.

Don't beat yourself up, because you ate one more doughnut. Eating is sometimes a reward for our behaviour or comfort for our pain.

Don't beat yourself up because you don't fit in. Some of us are built to stand out. When we mature, we begin to celebrate our uniqueness.

Don't beat yourself up because you don't like your creepy uncle. Trust your internal intuition and measure whom you like and whom you don't like. When we develop our intuition instead of denying it, we become wiser.

Don't beat yourself up because you do not have the courage to get out of bed today. No-one but you knows the burdens you carry. Most days, we can bear our burden and some days we just can't.

Don't beat yourself up because you cannot be all things to all people. We can't. We can only be who we are. Stop trying to please everyone - it's exhausting.

Don't beat yourself up because you feel fed up with your children. We know you love them, but some days they can test us beyond our limits. Love those days too.

Don't beat yourself up because you do not follow the belief system of your ancestral family. Sometimes life just leads us along a different path.

Don't beat yourself up because someone has made your diet, clothing, hairstyle and address, wrong. Guilt is such a wasted emotion.

Don't beat yourself up because you failed to get an education when you were young. Be an autodidact! Look it up, if you don't know what it means.

Don't beat yourself up. Society expects us to beat ourselves up for so many reasons. So many people are critical of us. Yet we beat ourselves up because of our own judgements the most.

Be kind to yourself.

STOP BEING A DICKHEAD PARTNER

19th June 2017

Dickhead partners are picky. They can pick. Any little thing gets picked at. They don't really know why they are picking, they just pick at absolutely everything: the way we drive, make the bed, take care of the baby, dry the dishes, mow the lawn or how we like to leave the toilet seat.

Both genders can do this - just about different things. They are not clear about what we must do to please them and they are just generally dissatisfied with everything we do. Eventually, we stop doing things for them and that is also a problem. If we are unclear about what it is we want or need, we become a picker. This will kill our relationships.

Find out what you want. If you are picking, you are probably behaving like your partner's parent, rather than their spouse. Nobody wants to have a romantically sensual relationship with their parent.

Dickhead partners are forever fixing things or giving advice. If he is painting or plumbing or cooking, for goodness sake stop telling him how to do it. If she is driving or drilling a hole or complaining about a colleague, for goodness sake stop telling her how she must do it right, or how to fix it.

When we are constantly told how to do things or how to fix things, we begin to stop communicating. This is very insidious and creeps into every sphere of communication. We stop communicating because we are always being told what to do or how to fix things. We don't want to be told what to do, nor do we need our partner to fix things for us. Being constantly told how to do things right infers that what we are doing is wrong – being told we are wrong all the time is exhausting.

We need to be heard. This is *not* just relevant to women. Both genders like to be appreciated, acknowledged and feel heard. Listen to your spouse instead of telling him or her how to do it or fix things. If he is changing the nappy, please let him do it!

Dickhead partners give the *silent treatment*. If you don't tell your partner why you are upset, then you don't have the right to sulk. *Still stuipe* (silent treatment) gives me the shits. Partners who do this are passive aggressive to the nth degree. This never serves our relationships.

If you can't tell your partner, in a decent and civilised way, why you are upset, then you are not emotionally mature enough to be in a relationship with a decent and emotionally mature human being.

MEMES CAN BE HURTFUL

20th June 2017

Women are responsible for creating memes that slate women. For example, "You're a cheap, good for nothing whore. That's why I love you." Or, "Bitch is doing it right!" or, "She's a tired old whore." We say terrible things to and about one another, and we laugh and enjoy it as a good joke.

Some of us set a ghastly example. Others observe our example, and memes like these are the result. Then those same women who disrespect and call other women names get upset when society adopts our attitude towards women.

Women are the first people to call other women names, or criticise their clothing, or blame them for their husband's roving eye. Women call other women names when their husbands step out. The guilty man does not get called names: just the woman.

When we as women begin to understand that *we* set the tone for how society treats women, then things might change. If you want attitudes towards women to change, change *your* attitude towards women. Do not call them names, do not criticise how they dress, do not make them feel small and do not treat them with disrespect. Do not share unkind memes on social media.

When we make how other women dress not okay, we make them wrong. The result of that is that when women lay rape charges, how they were dressed is used as evidence that they were wrong.

Women set the tone for society's social norms. We are the ones primarily raising the children. They hear what we say about other women. If we treat women with disrespect, how can we expect the attitudes of our children to be any different?

I get that the patriarchy plays a role, but it plays a bigger role because *we* make it okay to disrespect other women.

Give some thought to your own reactions if you see a woman you may feel is not appropriately dressed. Give some thought to your own attitude if you see a woman with too many children. Look at your attitude towards drunkenness. Is it any different if it is a woman or a man who is drunk? If you call a company and ask to speak to a more senior person, what gender are you expecting to answer your call? Have you called a woman a bitch or a whore? Have you blamed a woman when your partner has had an affair? Have you called that woman names? When in meetings, do you support other women?

If we change our attitude to each other, we will have a much bigger impact on society. Every time I see a woman post a meme on social media that criticises or makes another woman small, I cringe.

Statements like, "that time of the month" is as big as it is because we are okay with it. I wonder how many of us have thought about the violent incidents that are caused by testosterone. Men don't make their chemistry wrong. They think testosterone is as marvellous as their genitalia, of which they are so proud. We could learn from that.

I almost never hear one man say a bad thing about another man. If they have negative feelings, they keep them to themselves. But the women! We are so quick to make other women feel small.

Think of the impact we are having. If women start respecting women, we will have won half the battle.

ALL THE Q'S

22nd June 2017

IQ - Intelligence Quotient

This is our ability to work problems out and to understand things. This is purely an understanding capacity. Like understanding maths and *getting* things quickly. This has nothing to do with street smarts.

EQ - Emotional Intelligence Quotient

This is having mature emotional responses. Not using passive aggressive or manipulative methods to get what we need. This is the ability to be clear about what we want in order to feel happy and honouring what others want and need to make them feel happy and fulfilled.

SQ - Spiritual Intelligence Quotient

This is the ability to be connected to that which we believe to be divine. This is *not* religion. This is that feeling of awe we get when we look at a sunset, for example. When we are connected to that part of ourselves that has the capacity to feel awe, then we are connected to a higher part of ourselves. That higher part is where compassion, nurturing, non-judgement and unconditional love, or Agapé, resides.

PQ - Physical Intelligence Quotient

Knowing what your body needs to operate at optimum levels and taking appropriate steps to get our body into peak condition – whatever that means for each individual.

Few of us score high on all four Q's. I have a huge amount of respect for people with high EQ. They are the ones who are capable of having fulfilling relationships - not just the romantic kind.

Irrespective of the Q's - above all else - just be kind.

LIFE IS SO SHORT

23rd June 2017

Today, as I yet again attend a funeral, I am reminded that life is short. We think we have time, and that we can do it tomorrow. Sometimes, there is no tomorrow. We wake up and it is too late.

That friend you want to have coffee with, go and get it. That girl you want to phone to ask out, phone her. That phone call you want to make to your mom, make it. That fishing trip you are planning with your dad, book it. Those roses you want to send to your wife, order them. That ring you want to buy for your lover, buy it.

Some tomorrows never happen. We never know when the last time will be. When will we have that last kiss, that last phone call, that last cup of coffee, that last conversation?

We never know when it will be the last fish we catch or the last smile we can give a stranger.

Every time you have an argument with someone, consider that it may be the last words you ever speak to them. Life is too short to be angry and resentful, mean, and hateful.

Be kind. It may be the last opportunity you get

THINKING IS NOT DOING

25th June 2017

So many misunderstandings occur between friends and family because we *think* we are helping and the person who needs help thinks we are ignoring them. We spend a great deal of time in our heads worrying and thinking about a person who needs help. We may be spending a great deal of time thinking about how we can help and perhaps planning what we will say when we next see them, or what we will do when we see them.

From our perspective, we are spending a great deal of energy on the person and their problem, but they don't know this. It is not something of which they are even aware. We think they must know how much we care because they occupy so much of our headspace. But they don't. They only see what we *do*, not what we think we do.

By the time we connect to the person we love, we think they must be aware of how much of our time is consumed by our love for them. But they don't. All they see is the time we spend in their presence. The calls we actually make to them. The visits we actually show up for.

The invitations we actually extend. The meal we actually make.

Our loved ones get upset when they don't hear from us, irrespective of the amount of time we spend thinking about them and loving them from afar. This does not serve the person who needs us. By the time we eventually see them, we have had so many conversations running through our heads, that we have already had the conversations by ourselves - that we should have been having with them.

We then fail to hear our loved ones, because we believe we have already had those conversations. We fail to establish what our loved one needs or wants from us. We give what *we* feel they need, rather than establishing what it is that they, in fact, need or want. We feel that we have done much more than we have in reality because of the enormous amount of time we have dedicated to our loved ones in our heads.

Don't dismiss the energy of our intent. We are all sensitive to energy, even those who believe they are not sensitive. Our bodies are acutely aware of energy. And if we take a call from our loved one and we are slightly irritated or too busy, they can feel it. How often do we respond with irritation? This irritation causes our loved one to stop calling us because we are emitting this energy of irritation and, as a result, they feel that they are bothering us. Our loved ones will withdraw from us even more and feel even more isolated.

One of the most neglectful things we can do is fail to establish what someone needs or wants from us. What do *they* need to *feel* loved? We give what *we think* they want or what we think is good, or right, or appropriate, for them. Very often the two are not the same. If our loved one fails to be grateful for the help we have offered, we become resentful and we wonder why we help at all. Both parties are left saddened by the interaction. Sometimes, tempers can even flare up.

Our loved ones want our time. This is universally true. If we don't give them our time, we are not giving anything. And the time we spend thinking about them in our heads does not count. We are not *with* them. We are not present in their lives. We are not in their company.

When someone you love is taking strain, don't just talk about it and think about it. Be there. Get in your car and go there. Pick up the phone and call them or message them. Please be sure to give your loved one what *they* need and want, rather than what *you* think they should have.

Imagine if they got a phone call or text from us every time we fret and worry about them. Imagine how loved they will feel. Thinking about a loved one and worrying about a loved one serves only our conscience: it does not serve our loved ones.

Be there. Go there. Hear them. Send messages. We never tire of hearing that we are loved.

Never!

ACKNOWLEDGE WHAT IS SO

27th June 2017

In the new madness of constantly staying positive, we have forgotten the value of acknowledging what is so. Masking what is so under the guise of positivity does not serve the individual.

Khalil Gibran says, "The deeper that sorrow carves into your being, the more joy you can contain." Denying our trauma and pain is counterproductive to our learning.

In the age of staying positive, we fail to allow ourselves to surrender to our deepest sorrow. We put up a brave face so others may not think we are weak or negative. But this pain will come out. If not now, then later. If we cover our trauma and pain with a veneer of positivity, it will lie inside, fester and grow, until it erupts and cleanses itself in the light.

Don't hide your pain. Let it out. Show it to yourself and the world, that we may learn to honour each other's experiences once more. Allow others to hold you and care for you. Ask for what you need in your hour of darkness. Honouring the yin and the yang, the positive and the negative, the darkness and the light - it is never one thing you see. It is always two sides of the same coin. The one cannot be if the other does not exist.

We have become so blasé about our endless positivity and our endless pseudo happiness that we have no idea how to be there for each other when we lie broken in a puddle on the floor. But our brokenness can only ever last as long as it lasts and, inevitably, we will rise again. The wheel of life will never cease to turn. It is only when we truly experience our darkness, that we can celebrate our light.

Some days it is just too hard to get out of bed. Other days we jump out of bed in delight of this world - and this is as it should be. Without the one, we cannot appreciate the other. It is only ever love that gets us out of our deepest, darkest moments. No mantra, or verse, or admonition, or gift will get our spirits to lift once more. Only love. Love makes us whole again. And that is why we have to have people around us. We cannot live in isolation. We need love and compassion to thrive.

Ride your rollercoaster with pride, be broken when you are, and rise to your own glorious self when you are whole again. Love every part of who you are.

HOW CAN WE MAKE A DIFFERENCE

30th June 2017

Be the witness to those close to you. Truly acknowledge and *see* them. Instead of giving mindless advice or telling them how things should be done, be the witness. Tell them instead that you see what they are feeling or doing. Acknowledge what they are experiencing, whether that experience is joyful or sad. Simply acknowledge it.

We are all constantly bombarded with information. We get advice from so many sources and we are constantly told what, how, when and where to do and feel things. There is a solution and a recommendation for everything. Yet, we are all doing our best. We do everything we can. I know women always say we wear many hats because we are mothers, caregivers, home keepers, and career-minded. I feel that we do not acknowledge the men enough.

Men also wear many hats. They are fathers, husbands, fixers of broken things, takers out of insects, protectors, councillors, and often breadwinners. They do many unacknowledged little things besides the big ones that they do. Who has their backs? If we acknowledge what our men *do* for us, I guarantee they will do more of that. Acknowledge what they do, rather than point out what they don't do. This works - I promise!

We do not acknowledge each other often enough. Be the witness rather than the advice-giver. Tell your loved ones that you *see* what they do and feel.

The next time you are tempted to tell someone what or how to do or feel about something, or to point out what is *not* done, become still instead and look your loved one in the eyes. Tell them that you do notice what they do, or that you *see* what they are struggling with, or share their joy - even if it is a tiny thing. Acknowledge them and be a witness to their lives. Be the witness and see with your heart, not just your eyes.

Miracles will occur. I tell you truly that miracles will occur in your life.

THE NEW SPIRITUAL DOGMA

1st July 2017

If you think saying mantras or chanting or any other quick fix activity is going to release you from karma, you are delusional. It is exactly the same as asking forgiveness for sins. Dogma, is dogma, is dogma. The only way to stop karma is to stop being an idiot. All true spiritual messages are messages of love. Not mindless infatuation but true, compassionate love. Care of yourself and others. Make a difference in the world. *Here and now*. We are indeed our brother's keeper.

I saw a statement earlier today that an organisation is promoting *fighting for peace*. That is simply not possible. If you have to *fight* for peace, it can never be attained. We have had about 5000 years of recorded history and all the wisdom teachers have been telling us that *love* changes everything. For 5000 years we have known and have been taught that only love can change anything. Clearly, we are the slowest learners in the universe.

Yet, we still believe that we can ask a *God* outside of ourselves to make us more loving or more peaceful or to make the world a better place. Humanity is nuts. If we are behaving like idiots and killing people, raping, stealing, corrupting and harming the environment, how can we think that we can ask a God of any religion to change things on our behalf? It is we who are making those dumb and destructive decisions and only we can change things.

No God can change anything - we have free will. I can only imagine the various Gods sitting with their hands in their hair in despair, sadly shaking their heads.

God cannot fix human insanity. We can fix human insanity. We can stop being idiots. We continue to justify our behaviour by saying that others also behave like idiots and we will only change if they change first.

Be kind. Love thy neighbour. Respect others, even if you are the only one on the planet doing that. If you are not kind and compassionate and you are justifying your bad behaviour because others are idiots, you are compromising your own principles and sacrificing your authenticity.

If we are outraged by the behaviour of others and we behave in an outrageous way in retaliation, our world will never change, no matter how much we pray to and beg our various Gods to bring peace to our world.

JUDGEMENT AND ANGER

3rd July 2017

I have been told I judge, and I am angry. The person suggested that unconditional love is part of an enlightened person's spiritual practise and that a truly enlightened soul would not be so judgemental and angry.

Saying what is so is very different from judging something. Saying someone beats his wife is not judging them; it means that he beats his wife. Wanting him to change is judgement.

I am not capable of unconditional love for an individual who beats his wife or rapes a baby. I just am not. I am in a physical body with a brain that is hard-wired for flight or fight. I am simply not capable of unconditional love in these situations.

Bless those who claim they are. I am aware that there are masters on the planet who have the capacity. In all my 60 years, I *think* I have been in the presence on one master. And we all know that even Jesus got angry.

Now let's deal with anger. Anger is what changes the world. Outrage is what makes things different.

Unconditional love is the function of your soul. Your soul has no ego and therefore has *no capacity* to judge. Your soul is forever tethered to God consciousness, which also has no ego. There-fore, in our quietest moments, such as when we are in prayer or meditation, we can, for a brief moment, experience a glimmer of unconditional love, or Agapé.

Thank goodness for that. That is what keeps my head from exploding at the unfairness of this world. This planet is not a planet of unconditionality. It cannot be. It is a planet of polar opposites. We are here to learn what we are not before we can grasp that we are pure light and unconditional love. But I am not there yet.

I am not enlightened. If I were, I would know how to conjure food from the ether and turn water into wine, heal the sick and raise the dead. I have learnt and taught people about spirituality for a long time — although I prefer to call them wisdom teach-ings now. I still know that what I teach is not new, nor is it anything but common sense.

I love sharing my common sense, even sometimes when I am angry and outraged by what is going on in our world. I know that the *only* way we can change what is happening in our world is to change the way *we* live in it.

We change the way people do things or the way they behave by the example we set. Not by what we say.

EMPATHY

4th July 2017

"Empathy has no script. There is no right way or wrong way to do it. It's simply listening, holding space, withholding judgment, emotionally connecting, and communicating that incredibly healing message of 'you are not alone.'" Brene Brown.

This is by far the best description of empathy that I have ever encountered. Thanks, Brene. In our fast-paced, quick-fix society, there is little space for empathy, and yet it is sorely needed.

We all feel better when we meet up with that rare person who brings the gift of empathy.

Be that person.

HAVE WE LEFT THE MEN BEHIND?

4th July 2017

How have women grown over the last 40 years and have the men followed? I'm specifically referring to my generation's men and women. I observe that women have emancipated themselves. They run businesses, buy homes, travel extensively, and make a myriad of decisions every day.

They are no longer tethered to a time when a man was the provider and she the home-maker. Women of my mother and grandmother's generations had far fewer options than women of our generation.

We are, without a doubt, the mould breakers. We are the generation who insisted that we could have a career. Today's generation does not even question that. The women's liberation movement has highlighted that women are as capable as men and can, and do, achieve high goals and huge successes.

However, I find that fewer of my generation's men have kept pace with the fact that women are liberated. My father and grandfather pretty much spoke to my mother and grandmother as if they were slow children, as if things such as home finance and car insurance seemed a bit difficult for the average women to grasp back then.

Today a male friend asked me, "When you sold your house in Pretoria, did you invest that money?" My relationship with him is nowhere near close enough to even have such a conversation. I mumbled under my breath. He said, "You don't sound convincing. I'm worried about you now." I wonder if he would have had the same conversation with a male friend of his peerage.

I wonder how many men of my generation even know that they do this. I don't think they understand how often we are spoken to as though we are slow children. I was even recently told by a man of my generation that it is very unattractive for a woman of my age to swear. Not that it bothered me in the least whether he found me attractive or not.

I'm not bringing this up to be superior. I'm bringing it up because I genuinely believe that the guys are not aware that they do this. I do not find a benevolent, reprimanding, disapproving, complementary father figure sexually or romantically attractive at all. I certainly would not consider a serious date with such a man, let alone a little late-night dilly-dallying. He goes straight into the friend zone, and that is if he is lucky.

Don't even get me started on the way we are supposed to look. I overheard two men of my generation sitting in a restaurant discussing women as they walked past. They discussed the women and said that this one was a fixer-upper and that one could do with new boobs and the other needed to shop in better stores.

Neither of them was Adonis.

LIFE PURPOSE

6th July 2017

Many people that I have met over the last 30 or so years have yearned to know their life purpose. Some have found it and others simply do not care. Some are artists, some are musicians, some are engineers, some are doctors, some are lawyers, some are healers, and some are environmentalists.

It does not matter what you choose as your life purpose. The ultimate purpose is to live it with joy and to allow others to have whatever life purpose they choose.

I channel a teacher called Michael. No, not the Archangel. My Michael is just an ordinary person who lived many lifetimes on earth. He says that this is the third time that an independently mobile ensouled species has brought this planet to the edge of extinction. He also says that the planet itself is conscious and it is on its own evolutionary journey. Part of that journey is to accommodate independently mobile ensouled species.

However, if the planet's evolutionary process is threatened by its independently mobile ensouled species, it will do whatever it takes to bring itself back into balance. There is no value judgment about how many individuals may have to die to achieve this. The planet will simply do whatever it needs to do to ensure that it continues to survive and evolve and experience whatever it has chosen to experience, i.e. its life purpose.

My philosophy postulates that everything we experience is, in fact, a holy trinity: positive aspect and negative aspect, two sides of the same coin, and eventually, mastery, or neutrality. Mastery is the ability to observe what is so and loving it anyway. Therefore, if we have to experience everything in its positive as well as its negative, then we have a moral dilemma.

For example; If you have a life purpose called *saving the dolphins*, then you will have to concurrently orchestrate its opposite - that being the abuse or attempted annihilation of dolphins. If they are not threatened, how will you have something to save?

If you have a life purpose called healer, you have to concurrently co-create sick people. If you have a life purpose called saving the environment, you have to concurrently co-create the destruction of the environment. And so forth.

I am aware that this philosophy is going to upset many *do-gooders*. I am not suggesting that we must not care about our environment — quite the opposite. I am aware that like energy attracts like energy and that the energy of anger attracts more of that. I do not avoid my own anger and outrage. It is part of my human experience. In my saner moments I can look at a very bad situation and think, "There but for the grace of goodness, go I".

As a human, I can rant and blame and be outraged. Yet, on a soul level, I am aware that everything is as it should be and if mother Earth, or Gaia, feels overwhelmed by this parasitic independently mobile ensouled species, she will bristle and shake and ensure her own survival.

Michael says, "The most embarrassing thing a group of souls can do is blow up their own planet." I think we are getting close to that.

WHAT IS THE REAL PURPOSE OF ROMANTIC LOVE

7th July 2017

It is a safe haven for us to return to every night.

It is when we know someone has our back.

It is acknowledging that only one of us can fall apart at any given time.

It is where we place our first loyalty.

It is a place where we can share our true fears without concern that we will be ridiculed.

It is a place where we can laugh until it hurts.

It can lead to full body ecstasy.

It is the ultimate sense of belonging.

It is our go-to solution for all our problems.

In a world full of doubt and stormy emotional seas, it is our safe harbour.

It is where we can prove that we know the meaning of respect.

It is where we find encouragement.

It is where we share joy.

It is where we feel safe.

It is where we learn that if it resides in our hearts, it will remain manifest between us.

I wish to be aware of what resides in my heart - always.

I wish for only, honour, respect, support, encouragement, joy, and above all, love, to reside in my heart.

THE NEW DIVINE MASCULINE AND DIVINE FEMININE

9th July 2017

Oh, how I long for my feminine self to feel safe in this world; how I long to walk in freedom without fear of being harmed. This fear is real, and it is prevalent and pervasive.

I long to surrender once more to the Goddess inside. That Goddess is not weak. She is strong and she is vibrant. She is confident in her femininity, her natural intuition, her mystery, and she has an inborn desire to nurture and to care. I long for her creativity and divine healing energy. I long for her vulnerability and sensual radiance, her tenderness and patience. The feminine body with its fluid movement and soft, luscious shape. I want her back.

I learned long ago that I was imprisoned and that I wanted to be free, and I thought financial liberation would bring me that freedom. It did not. Financial liberation only taught me how to exist in a masculine world and I sacrificed my feminine self to achieve that freedom.

Yet, I am empty and barren, because the Goddess inside has to hide from the world of the masculine. I learned to be passionate, independent, disciplined and confident. I learned to be strong, logical and focused. Yet, I sacrificed my deepest desire. My desire to surrender, which does not mean to give up, it means to yield. But I can only really surrender if I feel safe. It is because I did not feel safe that I surrendered the Goddess instead.

Now I have a dilemma. The Goddess is looking out through the veil of protection that I have created around her. I have learned to keep her safe. But she is alone. The Goddess wishes to be a Goddess, for that is who she is.

She is looking for her God, her masculine counterpart, the one from whom she need not run and hide in fear. How I long for the safety of his embrace. There is nothing quite like the feeling of safety in his masculine embrace. But he is also hiding.

He has been blamed and shamed and made wrong. He is told that he is selfish and violent and not good enough. He has been told that he is not needed and that I can do anything he can do. And we are reminded in the words of Arun Eden-Lewis, that equality is not sameness. We are not the same and thank the gods for that. So the divine masculine has withdrawn and created the MGTOW (men going their own way) movement because that is where he feels appreciated and acknowledged.

We yearn, and we weep, we blame, we want, we seek, we desire, and we fail. We fail because we have forgotten that we are Gods and Goddesses.

I do not wish to play in the divine masculine world any longer. I wish to invite you into the softness of my divine feminine. Do not confuse my divine feminine to be a servant to your divine masculine – we are equal and different. I can only surrender to your divine masculine if I feel completely safe. And I know you can only come into my world if you feel respected.

"A woman's highest calling is to lead man to his soul so as to unite him with source. A man's highest calling is to protect woman so she is free to walk the earth unharmed." I don't know whose quote this is, but I would love that experience.

WHO AM I

15th July 2017

Recently, a woman on social media commented on something I wrote, "Just because you have written *one* book, does not make you God."

It certainly does not. In my view of the world, we are all here to share our experiences with each other. Sharing mutual experiences is what makes us feel as though we belong. I do not think that I have met anyone, ever, whose view of the world remains static. As we learn and mature, and have greater and more experiences, our view of the world changes.

I have always said there is no ultimate truth, there is only our perception of it and this perception changes as we grow and mature. Mostly, the stuff I wrote about 20 years ago is still the same: the fundamental message being love. I have also always claimed that the stuff I write about is aspirational and that I aspire to be the best I can possibly be. I have never hidden my dark side, the side that can get angry and outraged and pissed off.

I believe that there are people who are just wired to bring others *down a peg or two*. I believe they think that this will make others humble. The opposite of humility is pride and we as human beings swing quite comfortably between the two opposite poles. The opposite of judgment is acceptance, and this again is reflected in almost everything that we do, depending yet again on our perception of truth and where we currently sit on the pendulum's swing.

I, for example, have no need to bring others *down a peg or two* when they are being arrogant. However, put me in front of a stupid, obtuse person, and I lose my shit entirely. Our triggers are different depending on our perception of the truth. My ego wants to rush about and justify why I do not really believe I am God. My arrogance wants to let my tongue loose on the individual and let my sarcastic bitch emerge and then I can bring *them* down a peg or two.

Alas, I hope to remain sane and centred and not to let it affect me. I manage to do that *some* of the time. I aspire to allow myself to see their truth reflected in my desire to take revenge. If I am connected to my highest self in that moment, I can let it go.

If I am in pissed off human mode, I want to chop heads off and spit fire. That is the eternal yin and yang, the darkness and the light, the sweet and the bitter, the love and the fear.

And that is what makes us human.

SHAME

18th July 2017

Many of us live with deep-seated shame.

I have come across it so often whilst coaching people and it was, and still is in some instances, a factor in my own life.

Many have shame around money and very often feel ashamed about not having enough of it, or not being successful by current financial standards.

Some of us may be contributing to society in ways that are not commercially valuable. Many people I know are tender-hearted and conscious of the suffering in the world. They have very little but what they have, they share with others. Some of those tender-hearted people suffer hugely with shame.

Some of us simply do not fit in the world as it is currently structured. The painters and the poets, the healers and the givers, the naturalists and the environmentalists are the ones who contribute hugely and often for very little, or sometimes, no financial reward.

Then we have the teachers and the nurses. There was a time when these professions were prestigious, but now we as a society have diminished their value. We pay our sport and movie stars an obscene amount of money, but our nurses and our educators are at the bottom rung of the income scale. I know that most teachers spend a great deal of their own money on teaching aids because they do this job for heart reasons, not purse reasons.

I know many *tinkerers,* those people who are in their garages and workshops tinkering around. Imagine what they could invent if their basic needs were met? Or the helpers? Imagine how much more the helpers could do if they did not have to worry about working at dead-end jobs just to meet their basic needs. Imagine how many more volunteers we'd have?

I really want the world to provide to every human being the basic necessities of life. I want those with big hearts to feel proud of their big hearts so they may keep on giving and still be secure and safe in the knowledge that we honour them with shelter, food, clothing, and medical care. All are, as far as I am concerned, basic human rights,

If everyone felt safe, the world would be a better place. Imagine, just imagine, how much in the world would change if everyone had their basic needs met. I know there will be those who say that the world does not owe anyone anything. I disagree. I know there is enough in the world for everyone. I know that everyone can be fed if we just consider the amount of food that the industrialised nations throw away. If we were to spend less on wars and more on caring, the world would be a better place.

If we provide the basics for everyone, it will not change the commercial environment; we will still have those who work smarter, harder and seek more. I have met many poor people and yes, it is true that some of them just sit around doing nothing, but many poor people are some of the hardest working people I have ever met. Many others will still want the big house on the hill. That will not change. There is a huge difference between working hard and being commercially and financially successful.

Some countries are now working toward giving every citizen a minimum basic income so that they can afford the basics. I honour those countries. The result of that is a happier and more productive society with far less crime.

If we do this, there will be less shame. I know how it feels to be ashamed, ashamed that I am *not making it* in our financially driven world. I know that I feel more confident when I am able to pay my bills. I am free to make other decisions regarding my life if I am released from the bondage and shame of not being able to pay my way. When I am financially secure and my basic needs are met, I am more productive, I am happier, and I contribute much more to society if I am financially free. It is the same for most people.

Imagine a world where the basic needs of everyone are met? Imagine?

OFFER PRACTICAL HELP

8th August 2017

Praying for someone is really wonderful. Just as is sending love and light. Different words with the same meaning. Thank you for praying and sending love and light to someone.

Although it is much better if you actually pitch up with soup or cleaning materials and a bucket, or even a cup of tea. Pitching up and pitching in is what is required when someone is taking strain. Praying and sending love and light — while great — is neither very practical nor very helpful.

I wonder what Jesus or your Guru would say if, when you get to heaven or Nirvana, you are asked, "So, how did you help Jack when he was broke and homeless?" and you say, "I prayed for him and sent love and light."

Showing up and being physically present makes a huge difference in anyone's life. Actually, *being present* is the only way that we can help. We can't help by giving advice or by saying something like, "Why don't you send your CV out to as many companies as possible?" They probably already did that. What you could do is send their CV to *your* contacts! That is both practical and helpful. We can't help by pointing out the obvious. I was told, "Do you know that it is very important that you get a job because without a job you will never be able to pay your bills." As if this had never occurred to me in my 60 years of life.

Show up. I know you are busy. The only way we can help anyone is by showing up. Even if we show up and just allow someone to cry in our arms, that will help. They will know that someone cares enough to have taken the trouble to actually show up!

RELATIONSHIP KILLER

18th August 2017

Parenting your partner

If you speak to your partner as though you are their parent, they have no choice *but* to behave like a child. Stop parenting. Mothering them into oblivion makes for a crappy sex life.

Men do the authoritarian, disapproving, parent thing with their partner and it brings the same result. I get chills down my spine when I hear women say that their husbands are like their children. I just know that they speak to their husbands in dulcet *mommy tones*. It makes me cringe. I listen to the men who patiently speak to their wives as though they are a slow-witted child, or reprimand them for something that they may have neglected to do. I just know that there will probably not be any great sex in that house.

I know you mean well but stop - just stop. It is just not sexy. If you are in doubt about whether you use parenting communication style with your spouse, ask yourself if you would speak those same words or use the same tone of voice when you speak to your same-gender roommate?

Words like:

Why must you always...?

Why can you just...?

Why do I always have to...?

Can't you see that...?

You never...

Look hard at yourself in the mirror of your life and see how you behave towards your partner at a party or in public. Do you tell funny stories that are not flattering about your partner? The same type of stories and in the same tone of voice you use when you tell amusing stories about your cute or naughty kids?

One of my personal favourites... "Don't you think you have had enough to drink?" Or, "Why must you always tell those silly jokes?"

Parenting our partners destroys our relationships.

It is just not sexy.

THE LIES WE LIVE

22nd August 2017

I have read so many posts and memes on social media about lying and how many of us *hate* lies and liars.

Yet, most of us lie and we do it a great deal. Every time we say something that we do not mean, we are lying. For example, if someone asks us how we are and we say, "I'm fine," when we are in fact not fine, we are lying.

This has become so common that we already joke about what a woman means when she says she is *fine*. Sometimes we say something like, "It's no trouble at all," when, in fact, it is a great deal of trouble. Saying anything we do not mean is a lie. If our friend asks us to go to a movie with her and we make an untrue excuse about why we can't go, we are lying.

This constant lying has permeated every aspect of our society. It is so rife that we no longer even know what we really want because we are so used to lying. We lie because we think we are being diplomatic or saving someone's feelings. But, and this is a *big* but, when we lie, we are out of integrity with ourselves. Being out of integrity with ourselves is detrimental to our relationships, self-esteem and even our health.

When we lie, we feel unheard. This leads to feeling unhappy, resentful and discontented, which leads to argumentative and critical behaviour that destroy our relationships. Those lies sit in our reality and contaminate our lives. Our bodies know when we are lying and our bodies also know when another is lying.

I am not suggesting that we begin to be ruthlessly truthful. Actually, I am, but I recommend that we find a way to be truthful and still respect the other person and, ultimately, still remain kind.

In our society, we have learned that to say no is considered rude. However, saying no is not rude. It is perfectly acceptable to say no. We just have to learn not to be offended when another says no.

Perhaps we need an example. A friend phones to ask if we want to go to the movies. Instead of lying to get out of it, try this: "Thanks so much for the invite. I really do not feel like going to see movie X. But please do not stop inviting me. I really love your company." This keeps us in integrity with ourselves and does not offend our friend.

We joke about saying things we do not mean but, seriously, it serves no-one when we are out of integrity with ourselves.

INAUTHENTIC BEHAVIOUR AND PSEUDO PERSONALITY

24th August 2017

Over the years, as we grow up and mature, we experience fear, drama, anger, hatred, love, approval, disharmony, pain, and a myriad of other experiences. Our brain processes and stores these experiences. It forms a pattern where it anticipates the result or outcome of an experience.

Say, for instance, that we had a rough period of discontent and bickering with our mom. The brain begins to establish a pattern that recognises the pain of that interaction. This pattern then triggers a response based on past experience rather than the current situation. Therefore, our hackles literally rise before we actually have an interaction with our mom. We react based on past experience rather than the current situation.

Not only do we form patterns of behaviour that trigger certain responses, but we also learn how to avoid certain situations, or alter our behaviour to accommodate those situations. For example, we may begin to feel that if we are our normal loud, vibrant selves, people will judge us and then we change our personality to become more reserved and quieter. We may do this because we may feel that quieter people are more acceptable in a specific social environment, be that school, home, work or play.

This behaviour becomes habituated and although our natural personality may be loud and fun, over many years we may have dampened that down to be more conservative and quieter. We tend to do this around many aspects of our personality, and we alter our behaviour to suit the situation. However, in this process, we begin to forget who we really are.

Many years later, specifically around mid-life, we become reflective and begin to wonder who we really are. We become discontented with the pseudo-personality that we created in order to conform to society's idea of who we should be. Some of us — the lucky ones — begin to understand that we no longer need to invoke that pseudo-personality and we strive to become who we truly are. This is a great metamorphosis and, as with any metamorphosis, the process can be very painful.

When we begin to dismantle the pseudo-personality, people we have known for many years may say something like, "I don't know who you are anymore." Or, "You are not the person I married." This is, in fact, true. When we become our authentic selves, others often object to the change. Not because they disapprove, but because they have only ever met and interacted with our pseudo-personality. This will either cause a complete breakdown of our relationship or will deepen it to a whole new level.

This deepening can only happen if *both* parties are aware that we have lived from the perspective of the pseudo-personality. Michael calls this pseudo-self, false personality or Maya. If both parties were to become their true authentic selves, this would bring much liberation to our lives.

I have worked really hard to become my authentic self. My pseudo-personality is very much alive and well. This self-work has liberated me from worrying about the opinions of others, both good and bad opinions. It did take a long time though, and my pseudo-personality fought this metamorphosis tooth and nail to defend itself from its own demise. Our pseudo- personality, like everything else, just wants to remain alive. Therefore, we may regress easily into old, habituated behaviour patterns that do not serve our authentic self.

As long as we are aware of this regression, we can actually work on it. Our pseudo-personality was created to protect us from hurt. Therefore, we need to honour it and invite it into our authentic reality, knowing that it has served us well. There is nothing quite as liberating though, as knowing who we really are and behaving and reacting from our true, authentic self. This brings us to a whole new level of love, honour and respect, both for ourselves and others.

The downside, of course, is that we know when others are still grappling with their pseudo-personality. We know this because our bodies can easily identify inauthenticity. It often feels as if the person with whom we are dealing is dishonest or is lying. This is not the case.

It would be much more beneficial if we looked upon those still grappling with a false personality and say, "There but for the grace of God go I," rather than judge and condemn.

PAIN MAKES YOU STRONGER

1st September 2017

Pain can and often does make one more resilient but it can also break us. Relentless physical or emotional pain is exhausting and I doubt that it makes us stronger. It takes a little bit more from us every time pain causes havoc in our lives. Some of us cope with the pain of everyday life and some of us succumb to the pain and give up, and some may even commit suicide.

If it were true that hardship makes people stronger, then the strongest people must be the very poorest of us. I have been to India; I have seen the poorest of the poor and I have seen the pain of their suffering. The statement that it makes us stronger is one of those damn platitudes that is designed to make us feel better about the crap that we are going through.

It is something someone throws out at us because we do not know how to empathise with each other. We do not know how to face another's pain and we create platitudes that we toss in the social mix — but they never work.

This whole journey of staying positive and looking at the bright side is a platitude that we throw out to make us feel better in the face of our own and another's sheer tragedy and pain.

If we ignore our pain, and if we ignore our negative feelings, we can put a lid on it. It does not go away, it lies there — sometimes very deep inside us — and it festers and eats away at our self-esteem and courage.

Eventually, the pain will erupt and spew its tragedy all over our life. The pain will come out. If not now, then later.

I wish we were comfortable enough to allow each other the freedom to feel our pain. I wish we could hold sacred and safe space for another, which would allow others to feel what it is that they're feeling without the need to cover it up with a mindless platitude.

I wish we could create a more compassionate society, where the whole spectrum of human emotions is accepted. If only we were allowed to really feel our feelings, and if we could learn to express those feelings appropriately, and when we feel them.

To hell with platitudes and to hell with the look-on-the-bright-side bunnies. I will hold sacred space for you and allow you to fall apart and wait until you are ready to pick yourself up. I will not turn my face away from your pain.

I get that I could not face the world's pain all at once. I get that it would probably cause my body to self-combust. But I will hold sacred space for the people I care about and for those in whose life and can make a difference. I will not deny your pain by offering you a mindless platitude.

IS PRAYING FOR HEALING ALWAYS APPROPRIATE?

4th September 2017

Is it always appropriate to pray for healing, or to send healing light, prayer or energy? Personally, I do not really believe that there is any difference between them. They may be different words but have the same meaning and result, or purpose and intent.

My question then is, "Is it always appropriate to wish for healing for another?"

I don't think so. I have been faced with this dilemma. More than once.

I truly feel that we often pray for the healing of an individual because *our* lives will be thrown into despair if the person for whom we are praying leaves this mortal world. For me, praying or sending healing energy is not always appropriate. Let me give you an example. Let's say someone we love was involved in a serious accident and they are in a critical condition in a coma in hospital. We want our loved one to recover. We pray for healing and wish for them to wake up and be with us once more. At the time we will be distraught, as the thought of our loved one dying distresses us deeply.

Yet, we give very little thought to the quality of life our loved one may have should they wake from their coma. I am aware of the intensity of our emotions during such a traumatic time since I faced this with my own child.

He was in a coma and had sustained head injuries as a result of an accident. With head injuries, doctors are often not able to give an accurate prognosis.

I made a decision to work with my son's soul and to engage with that part of him that is connected to his divine life path, irrespective of the emotional cost to myself. I would deal with the outcome no matter what that may have been.

I sat next to Clinton's bed whilst he was in a coma and suffering intermittent seizures. I asked his soul to be present with me. I called on all that is Divine and requested whatever was most appropriate for him and his soul to manifest for him at this terrible time. I asked that his soul, in conjunction with his divine will and his guardian angels, should decide what was appropriate for him in this moment, given the extent of his injuries.

This was probably one of the most difficult things I had ever done in my entire life. I told Clinton that it had been an honour being his Mom and that I would love him anyway and any way. I knew that he would either recover or die.

This process took several hours while I stayed in a prayer-like, meditative state. A complete calm came over me and I knew I was in the presence of divine consciousness. I knew that the appropriate choice would be made with regard to Clinton's healing, irrespective of my own feelings and desires. In that moment, I was fine with either outcome.

I was okay with it until I got home, and my normal human mind processed what I had truly asked for. I was so distraught at the thought of losing my beloved child.

On this occasion, my loved one recovered.

I have had another experience where the person I loved did not recover. In both instances, I applied the same principle.

Irrespective of our own desire for the health or healing of another, I believe that we should ask for that which is in alignment with our loved one's soul or divine choice.

I do not believe that it is always appropriate to pray or wish for healing, no matter how difficult that thought might be for us. Obviously, I am talking about life and death situations.

I know miracles happen: I have experienced one. I still believe that they happen in alignment with the soul's choice and the divine purpose of the individual.

I feel that those who may be fretting over the sick person can and do hold a soul in suspension here on earth. We hold the soul here because of our own deep grief at the thought of them leaving this mortal coil. I do not believe that it is always appropriate to pray for recovery. I know how hard this is.

Life at any cost can sometimes mean "less-than-life" in reality.

May you gain clarity when faced with tragedy and sadness. May you find peace. May you be guided to do what is in line with the divine purpose and soul choice of the individual who is ill.

May you find the courage to cope with the outcome, whatever that may be.

NOTHING WILL CHANGE UNLESS WE DO

16th September 2017

How is it possible that we do not know this? How is it possible that so many of us keep doing the same things we have always done and expect a different outcome?

If we are honest, we will see that all our relationships end in similar ways or have the same difficulties and challenges. If we are honest, we will see that all the fights we have are over the same things. If we are honest, we will see that all the old patterns emerge when the same buttons are pushed. We then expect others to change *their* attitude, or what *they* are doing so that our irritation levels are reduced. It is madness to do the same thing over and over again and to expect a different outcome!

We feel outraged when others gossip about us, yet we gossip.

We feel outraged if others are racist, yet we talk about others who are not like us with derision.

We feel outraged when others have bad manners. Yet if we step into their culture, our manners may be considered bad.

We get so offended if someone wears clothes that we deem inappropriate.

We insist on being right and that our way is the only way and we get so upset if others do not do what we do.

Yet, we will sprout forth that we love diversity. Crap! We don't. We make others wrong all the time. If we take a really hard look at what offends us so deeply and if we decide to let that crap go, the world will be a much better place.

If we make a decision today that we will not be offended by anything anyone else does — just for the day – we could perhaps imagine by what margin we can reduce our anger and irritation levels.

Many of us are constantly angry. We get angry because others are not doing what we want them to do. We are angry, we judge others, we lie, and we are offended a great deal of the time.

Ask yourself, "What do I need to make me happy?" I guarantee that most of us will know what makes us unhappy. Few of us know what makes us happy.

How can others give us what we need to be happy if we do not know what that is? Take your time. Work out what you want or need to be happy. Let go of most of the crap that offends you. I guarantee that you do not even really know why things offend you.

Once we have figured out what we really want, and have given up the need to be right and to be offended, our lives will be greatly changed and much more peaceful.

Once we *understand* this, we can learn to ask others what we need from them, rather than being offended because they are not giving us what we don't even know we need in order to be happy.

We don't even know that we don't know what we need to be happy.

WE GIVE TO OTHERS WHAT WE WOULD LIKE TO RECEIVE

18th September 2017

This rarely works as well as we intend. We give to others that which we feel we would love to receive. This happens in such a subtle way that we do not even know that this is what we're doing. We then get offended if the recipient of our *kindness* is not appreciative of our gift.

Let's take a look at how this typically works. Let's say that carrots are our newest, most favourite cure-all or passionate pursuit. We sprout forth about the benefits of carrots and how important it is for everyone to eat carrots all the time, or how much we love this new passion of ours and how beautiful carrots are.

Our friend may have a birthday and we give her carrots for her birthday. She receives the carrots less than enthusiastically. We are offended because we really want her to understand the importance of carrots and what they mean to us, and we need her to gush as enthusiastically about carrots as we do.

We give to others what we would want to receive. Obviously, I used carrots only as an example. Let's look at another example.

Perhaps family is most important to you and perhaps you have a lovely family and enjoy spending as much time with them as possible. You may have a friend, let's call her Cheryl, who is not as close to her family. You do everything in your power to get her to spend more time with *her* family because you know how happy you are in the company of *your* family. You even orchestrate that you phone Cheryl's boyfriend and say something like, "You should really encourage the family to visit Cheryl more. It is really important, and it is the right thing to do."

Perhaps you do not know the family circumstances or history. Perhaps Cheryl is tired of her family sponging off her or she is exhausted from dealing with their drama. Perhaps it suits her that she does not see her family so often. You may not know that there was a really tragic event that happened in Cheryl's life when she was a child and she is still dealing with the trauma of that experience.

Not only have you interfered in Cheryl's life, but you have made it the responsibility of another adult to ensure that Cheryl's family visit her. The other party is not responsible for healing the wounds between Cheryl and her family, and this third party may now feel guilty because they are not comfortable acting on your suggestion. Your intention may have been honourable, but there is a reason why we say the road to hell is paved with good intentions.

We project our needs and desires onto those around us and think they should be delighted that we want for them what we want for ourselves. Sometimes this may be true. But I find more often than not, it is not the case.

When we give to another that which we would like to receive in order for *us* to be happy, we get offended if they don't receive our gift with love and enthusiasm.

And God forbid if they say, "No thanks, I don't want this." Or God forbid if they tell us to stop interfering in their lives.

Perhaps they do not want what we are trying so very hard to give them, and with such good intentions.

More often than not, we don't even know that we are doing this. There is a very fine line between helping and interfering. My rule of thumb is that unless I hear the words, "Please help me," I do not offer advice or solutions or suggestions. I try to simply allow the person I am with to voice their feelings and hold space for them to do so without my advice or interference.

HEAVENLY HELPERS

27th September 2017

I have a huge amount of respect for people who help others.

Many people have good hearts and help where they can. Some dedicate their lives to helping. There do not seem to be statistics for shelters that I can find. I do know that I am inundated with pleas for help with animals every day. Animal shelters receive more money from the general public than do human homeless shelters.

I can't fathom why we continue to believe that humanity will treat its animals with more respect than we treat our own species. We continue to want to create more laws to protect animals, and yet we have many laws protecting humans and our prisons are full of humans who kill other humans or harm them in some warped way.

It is clear that laws don't change behaviour. Violence is increasing, not decreasing. Neither is the threat of hell stemming the flow of violence, which is why humanity created the concept of hell in the first place. If our very religions that are teaching peace, love and tolerance are threatening humanity with the utmost violence — burning in the everlasting fires of hell — then that threat of violence will filter through to our whole society.

Violence, you see, begets violence. Our animal protectors want to punish those who harm animals with violence — bless them.

We punish those who harm others with violence. We think discipline should include violence. And the violent merry-go-round continues.

We know that violence begets violence because our churches preach violence and our governments promote violence and, as a result, violence is prevalent. Our governments can only really promote violence because the highest spend on most of the world's government budgets is earmarked to further promote arms manufacture and warfare, rather than peace.

I wonder sometimes if the message preached by the churches did not instil fear, would anyone still go to church? I will tell you who has stopped going to church. The 2% of the world's population who have evolved enough to begin to believe that love will make a difference. They have started an alternative movement. Those who have woken up and who have had enough of the oligarchy, the corporatocracy, and the kakistocracy are stepping out of the mainstream and they are seeking a different way.

If we do not begin to support projects like The Venus Project, (go on – Google it), which has a technologically advanced, peaceful, sustainable, inclusive, participative and caring philosophy, we, as a species are doomed, and rightly so. The 2% who have woken up and who are attempting to change the world is not enough. More people need to join their ranks.

But we are small, isolated groups slogging at trying to awaken people to the power of love. If we can create a world where we teach love rather than violence as a solution to our problems, we may change our world. Even our Gods are wrathful and violent.

Separation, division and competition cause violence. Inclusion, co-operation and love do not.

Imagine how much more peaceful our world would be if every

human being had shelter, food, clothing and healthcare? This is what we require and demand for our animals. But God forbid we demand the same for our fellow humans. People lose their minds if one suggests that every human being is entitled to have their basic needs met. We do not have a problem demanding that for our pets though. Yet, we can't expect that for our animals if we don't consider it to be a basic *human* right as well.

HABITUAL NEGATIVE BEHAVIOUR PATTERNS

28th September 2017

I write about habitual negative behaviour patterns often. What are habitual negative behaviour patterns? These are communication patterns that have been formed and embedded in our consciousness over many years.

Let me share an example of one of mine. Habitual negative behaviour patterns are generally never pretty.

When I start a conversation with someone and I feel that the person to whom I am speaking is not going to understand the concept that I wish to convey, I instantly switch off my brain and no longer wish to continue to explain myself or my point. If an individual is discussing something in which I have no interest, my eyes literally glaze over and I go to another world.

I know this is arrogant and it makes me feel like a heel. I lose interest in the conversation and become bored. This, of course, is extremely discourteous to the individual in whose company I find myself. I have to guard against this very often and I am successful at stopping this behaviour *some* of the time.

From an energy perspective, the person to whom I am speaking can *feel* the energy that I project. They feel that my attention has shifted, and they can literally *feel* the disrespect. It is tangible.

We can rarely describe or understand this feeling. Our reaction to this feeling is intense. We do not really even know where this feeling comes from or why it is there, but we fully understand that something has made us uncomfortable and has put us on our guard. Sometimes we react to this feeling with violence, sometimes with passive aggression, but mostly, we just feel confused or hurt.

This same feeling is present when we do something for someone that we really do not want to do. We even project this inauthenticity when we do something for someone with the inadvertent need for approval, the need to be acknowledged or to be thought of as a good or nice person. An example of this is when we give the beggar at the traffic light some money or food expecting gratitude or thanks. We are giving with the intention to receive something in return: gratitude. We then become disapproving and angry if the beggar fails to display gratitude.

This feeling is also present when we grow up in our culture with certain rules, standards, or *manners*, and we take those rules and standards to be good and right. They become our measure of right and wrong. If anyone behaves in conflict with those standards, we emit a low level of displeasure and disapproval. We don't actually verbalise our disapproval or anger, we just hold it in front of us like a proverbial energy sword.

This could literally become a habitual negative behaviour pattern that we carry around with us day in and day out. The people around us can feel the emotion that we emit. They feel it and may even ask, "Is everything okay?" We may even smilingly respond that everything is indeed okay, but we continue to emit the feeling of disapproval and displeasure. This can be made physical by becoming silent and distant, or door-slamming, or variations of that kind of behaviour.

For the people around us, this constant energy of unidentifiable disapproval and displeasure is tangible, and they begin to walk on eggs. This is what passive aggressive behaviour feels like. Few of us understand that we are passive-aggressive. We are often passive-aggressive because society frowns upon open displays of aggression or violence. Passive aggression has become a perfectly acceptable social coping strategy and yet it is destructive in the extreme.

Passive aggression is very often the cause of many relationships ending in disaster. It is not as if there is a huge problem such as womanising or drinking or gambling or drugs. There is just this constant, low-grade disapproval and displeasure. When we live with this all the time, it is exhausting, for us as well as those around us. This constant disapproval and displeasure is a major cause of stress in our lives.

Of course, the solution is to recognise that we behave in this way. We could learn to acknowledge that we require something from the people in our lives, and we could learn how to verbalise that need. If we are upset at someone's behaviour, let's talk about it.

If we do not tell people what we need, how can we become disapproving and displeased because they're not giving it to us? We do not tell the people in our lives what we want because we don't actually know that we want in order to feel happy and content.

This is why I call our regular reactive response, 'habitual negative behaviour patterns;' it is subliminal and automatic. Yet, it is manipulative and exceedingly destructive.

If we are holding a feeling of constant disapproval and displeasure of others and what they do, and we get angry because they don't change their behaviour, we are participating in passive-aggressive behaviour.

We will have to retrain our brains to be able to function on a different level. That is the tricky part. Yet, if we don't do that, we will spend the rest of our lives in a cloud of displeasure and disapproval.

This, of course, serves no one. Least of all, ourselves.

RELATIONSHIP TROUBLES

4th October 2017

If your relationship at home is one that is conducted with the blame game, silent treatment, sarcasm, resentment, and disrespect, please do not be surprised if your partner ventures outside of your relationship to feel wanted and loved.

Please do not blame the other party that has captured your partner's interest. It's really rare for anyone to venture outside of their relationship for love and comfort if they are receiving that at home.

It is my experience that for a partner to venture outside of their relationship, there will have been an extended period of discontent and unhappiness. Bitching and moaning or blaming a third party and being outraged is not going to solve your problem. In fact, it will make it worse. It *always* takes two to tango. In my experience, it is never just one party's fault that a partner has stepped out. *Both* partners will have participated in on-going blame, silent treatment, resentment, and disrespect.

I have heard many women say that their partner stepped out, "After everything they did for them." I often ask, "Did you do all those things consistently, without resentment, or were you resentfully banging dishes and sighing whilst doing *all* of those things?"

If we do something for someone in order to get any kind of reward, we are not giving from a place of unconditional love. If we receive something that someone else is giving us and we show no appreciation, then we cannot expect the other party to continue giving.

Relationships go wrong because we spend years dabbling in the blame game, silent treatment, sarcasm, resentment, and disrespect. Therefore, when I see a partner blaming a third party for their partner's indiscretion, I just know that their relationship will have been in trouble for a long time.

Blaming a third party is completely pointless. If we stop participating in the blame game, silent treatment, sarcasm, resentment and disrespect, our relationships stand a much better chance of being fulfilling.

I'm not talking about rogues who will step out no matter what. That is the exception, rather than the rule.

THE GREAT QS

12th October 2017

IQ is the quotient of intellectual intelligence. The higher this is, the better we are at understanding things and increasing our ability to work things out. IQ brings critical thinking and problem-solving.

EQ is the quotient of emotional intelligence. This is the means by which we deal with relationships and feelings. The higher the quotient, the less we need to manipulate and hate. It brings maturity and emotional balance.

SQ is the quotient of spiritual intelligence. The higher this quotient, the less we need others to believe as we believe, and we no longer need to make another's belief systems wrong. It brings peace and harmony.

PQ is the quotient of physicality. This teaches us how to keep our bodies healthy and strong. The higher this quotient, the more aware we are of the damage we cause to ourselves and the planet as a whole. It brings fitness and health.

LQ is the quotient of love. This is not Eros or romantic love. This is unconditional love or Agapé. The higher this quotient, the more accepting we are of universal truths and the more compassion we have for all living things. It brings compassion and acceptance.

Some of us have more of one than the other. I have yet to meet anyone who has mastered all of the Qs. I guess, as we go along, we will define more Q's.

#METOO

19th October 2017

No. The #metoo project is not about a girl and a guy in the back seat of a car. It is not about a misunderstanding, innuendo and mixed signals. Not for me.

It is about that guy that cat-calls you on the street and you want to giggle but you ignore it because you *know*. He does not like being ignored and he grabs your arm, leaving bruises, and says, "You think I'm not good enough for you?" Or, "Are you ignoring me because I'm Indian?" "No, I'm ignoring you because you are a prick and I anticipated your reaction," we silently scream.

This is often a catch 22 situation. If we respond in any way, the situation could escalate. If we do not respond, the situation may escalate anyway. This kind of interaction may have been fun if it didn't escalate or lead to potential danger. Situations like this could turn nasty in an instant.

The #metoo project is about being a sales rep and a client suggests that he will only give me the large order if I go away with him for the weekend. Even worse, when I explain the situation to my boss, he says, "If the client wants you to go away with him, you will go, if you want to keep your job." You can complain to HR, but you're Just. Too. Tired. Of. It. All.

It's about the guy in the crowded lift who touches your arse. You knew he was going to do something because your radar was up. But if you moved away to avoid it, there could have been nasty repercussions.

It's about people saying, "I wonder if those are real?" I have had a double mastectomy with reconstructive surgery and this kind of statement really upsets me.

The #metoo project is about being alone in the house when you are twelve and your uncle arrives and pins you to the wall and sticks his hand up your skirt. When you scream, he holds you tighter and says, "Just wait a little bit, then you will like it." The next time your family visits this uncle, you don't want to get out of the car... and you get a hiding.

The #metoo project is about the guy in the shop who says, "If she smokes, she pokes," when you buy a packet of cigarettes, diminishing you as a sexual being.

It's about a husband who breaks your nose because supper was not on time or the coffee was too hot.

It's about being in the movie house by yourself and a guy comes and sits next to you. He takes his penis out and asks you to touch it.

#metoo is about being afraid to walk through the parking garage to your car if you see two men chatting in the distance because you just don't know if you will be safe or if you will be grabbed, touched and you feel helpless and unsafe.

It's about the teacher who asks you to stay behind after class and he touches your boob and tells you that you will get great marks if you show them to him.

#metoo is about your boss telling you that you will get a bigger bonus if you sleep with him.

It's about the church minister who helped you cope with a difficult situation and you trusted him. The next home visit he makes, you get that awkward feeling because he put his hand on your thigh and rubbed it up and down in a certain way. And you know! You just know that he is no longer there to help, but you feel trapped, afraid, unsafe, shocked and disillusioned — in your own home — and have nowhere to run. And you know that if you said anything, no-one would believe you because he *is* the pillar of your community.

It's about the relentlessness of these situations. And it is about women knowing this relentlessness and feeling desperate, helpless, afraid and unsafe.

#metoo is about the knowing look we give our sisters, daughters, friends, mothers, and aunts because we know that they know and feel helpless, hopeless, afraid and unsafe as well.

These are just a few of my #metoo moments and compared to what some women have had to endure, I am supposed to feel *lucky*.

#metoo is about *your* wife, daughter, mother, son, husband and uncle. It will not go away until the men step up and acknowledge that their behaviour needs to change. The #metoo project is not a women's issue. It is a men's issue.

IN THE MEAN TIME LIVING

24th October 2017

Many of us do it and we don't even know it. We pick a house and live in it in-the-meantime until we find a house we really like. We have in-the-meantime jobs, which we work at every day but only until we get the job we really want. We have in-the-meantime lovers, just until we meet that one perfect partner whom we will marry.

We live in-the-meantime for so long that our in-the-meantime life has become how we live our whole life. Then, one day, when we pay attention, our life has passed us by and we have not really committed to anything. Our in-the-meantime experience is a smokescreen we make for ourselves to justify why we don't need to commit. We don't need to commit to anything because this house, car, job, lover is not what we will settle for, ultimately. It is just for the time being or in-the-meantime.

We kid ourselves that this life we are living is not as good as it gets, right in this very minute. We don't really participate in our life ... well, because ... it is only in the meantime until we find the real thing. Then we will commit to living fully. Then we will be happy. And *then* we will give it everything we've got. In the meantime, though, this thing we have right now will do.

We know it is in the meantime living because we don't really want to ask her to marry us, because well... she is an in-the-meantime-girlfriend, and it is really too much trouble to end the relationship. In the meantime, years and years pass. She knows and I know that we are not committed — not really.

We know when we aren't in the right job. We know because we don't really enjoy it. It may not be a bad job but it isn't what we really want to do. So, we do nothing since it's an in the mean-time job and it pays well enough and we'll eventually get around to updating our CV. But for now, it will do.

We don't make a nice garden, because we don't really like the house we live in and why make a nice garden if we're going to sell it? Our little in the meantime house.

We date people because they are really nice. They are not 100% what we are looking for and we don't really know what we're looking for, so we will date this person, in the meantime. At least we have someone who can go to the movies with us.

So, we live an in the meantime life until we've been doing it for so long that now it's too late. We realise our life is passing us by and that this in the meantime nonsense is not really making us happy.

Commit. Commit to your life. Stop this in the meantime living. Make real decisions. Decide what you want and commit to it. If it is not what you want, and if it does not make you happy, change it.

THE INTERDEPENDENCE OF LIFE

1 November 2017

Way back, when we lived in villages, we had elders who helped guide our villages to be more peaceful, helped us to resolve our conflicts and taught us to co-operate with each other. Those elders knew that we were interdependent on each other. It has always been that way. Just because we live in an industrialised world, it does not mean that we are no longer interdependent, even though we feel we are super-independent. Independence suggests that we make our own decisions and are able to look after ourselves economically. While independence is to be lauded, interdependence remains a fact.

We rely on others to provide everything that we need: the grocer, the furniture maker, the farmer, the chef, the employer, the nurse, the cobbler, and the weaver. Just because we do not encounter each of those individuals personally anymore, it does not mean that we do not rely on them to provide for our needs.

When we go to a hospital, we may need a blood transfusion, yet we do not know where that blood comes from. When we own an aid organisation, we do not always know the people who contribute to our cause. Yet, we still help each other, even though we may not encounter the *helper* personally.

We do not know the gender, the language, the race or the age of the individual who has helped create or participated in the manufacture of the goods that we need and use. Nor do we know whose blood runs in our veins once we've had a blood transfusion. We don't even consider who has had to suffer because we eat chocolate, or the impact that has on the environment. We do not know who donated that grand piano to our orphanage or who works relentlessly behind the scenes to create our birthday party because mom did not have time and she subcontracted a woman to help her.

We know that we are interdependent on our nanny, employer, technician, welder, housekeeper, gardener, husband, parents, and many others, who we may actually encounter every day. All those people upon whom we are interdependent are not all like us. Some are of a different age and others have a different skin colour, and some may speak another language. And we are okay with that. We are okay with this interdependence in our daily lives.

I believe we have taken independence to a tragic level. This pursuit of utter independence has isolated us from those around us and has put distance between us and the people who make the stuff we need. Industrialisation is not all it is cracked up to be.

If we are honest, we will all admit that we yearn for that interdependence. An interdependence where our talents and contribution to the greater whole is rewarded with honour and respect and a place in the tribe. We no longer have a feeling of belonging. We are isolated in our independence and many of us have achieved much, yet we return to our empty homes in the evening and there is no-one who notices what we have achieved. It is truly an empty existence.

I want my village back.

THE DOGMA OF BELIEF SYSTEMS

14th November 2017

Any belief system that excludes others or makes a specific group special or more deserving is a crock of poo.

Every individual is on their own spiritual path. There is no other path to be on. There is only a spiritual path. There is no judgement of good and evil other than in the realm of the physical. Most holy books say something like, "There is nowhere that I am not." This refers specifically to God. That means that the divine spark is in everything and everywhere. Therefore, nothing and no one can possibly be excluded.

I just read the following in a *spiritual* article:

"Basic energy shift (ascension) symptoms included things such as ringing in the ears, intense sweating, dizziness, forgetfulness, ascension flu, depression, and waves of nausea. It seems that most people who begin the shift into a higher frequency experience these."

Ascension flu? Would one get that as a result of too much meditation, or too little medication?

You are in a physical body and science can explain the ringing in your ears and your dizziness as well as all the other so-called *ascension* symptoms.

I have been on this spiritual path for a long time now and all that I have learned is that people are talking about the same old tired concepts and giving them new names. Heaven and hell have become ascension and karma. Same sh*t, different day. We are special and you are not. We are right and holy, and you are unbelievers and wrong. Same sh*t, different day.

Being spiritual does not mean I have to change anything or do anything. Hopefully, being spiritual makes me a nicer person today than I was yesterday. It wakes us up to the wrong we perpetrate on others every day.

Hopefully, being spiritual makes me aware when I am being a dick and humble enough to say, "I stuffed up, I'm sorry."

Being spiritual does not make me arrogant, pious, prescriptive or anything else. It makes me self-aware and that means that I recognise when I am a dick.

Self-awareness teaches us that everyone including ourselves deserves a second and a third and a fourth chance.

SANCTIMONIOUS VEGETARIANS

23rd November 2017

My ranting about the sanctimonious behaviour of some vegetarians sparked off a huge debate on social media. The food debate is no different from the religious/spirituality debate. It is still one group of people making the other group wrong and saying that their way is the truth, the way and the light. And this discussion actually has nothing to do with food.

Interestingly, I come from a family of hunters and I seriously believe that if you hunt your own food, it is a great deal more humane than the way that we raise some animals for food. I am fully aware of the cruelty factor. Therefore, I cannot be hypocritical and say that I am opposed to hunting, and still eat the biltong or venison stew.

I recognise the complete pointlessness of trophy hunting but that is a different matter altogether. I'd be quite happy to eat lab-grown meat, but for my body type, the amino acids, besides just the protein, is critical.

I have tried being a vegetarian. After a year or so of vegetarianism, I went to my regular beauty parlour for a wax and bits of my skin came away with the wax.

This vehement opposition to meat eaters irritates me when people make value judgments about the choices of others. It ranks right up there with the people who are judgemental about breast implants. Some make those decisions for vanity and others do so because they have had mastectomies. Think before you judge.

I still find some vegetarians exceptionally sanctimonious...

I am vehemently opposed to anyone who makes the choices of others wrong. We are beings who re-incarnate and during our cycle of lives, we all do many atrocious things.

Besides, my view of the world is that if we have a life purpose called *saving something*, then we have to concurrently co-create that which needs saving. You cannot have a life purpose called save the dolphins, rain forest, street dogs or anything else if their demise doesn't exist.

Therefore, philosophically, from *my* point of view, if we are the saviour, we also have to co-create the perpetrator or the destroyer.

NAIVE IDEALISM AND BITTER REALISM

2nd December 2017

The swing of that pendulum is quite severe, and balance is truly required.

Naive idealism teaches us that the sun always shines. It wants us to stay positive in all things. It is that part of us that wants to tell our friends to look on the bright side even if they've just lost a leg by saying something like, "You're lucky, a friend of mine lost both of his legs in an accident." Or, those who say, "He will always be with you," when you've just lost the love of your life.

Extreme bitter realism is when we have just gone through a terrible divorce and we say all men are bastards — or much worse.

Neither is good.

If we are in naive idealism or in bitter realism, we are not feeling our true feelings as we experience them. Those who are around us, who are stuck in either extreme spectrum of the pendulum swing, will want for us what they want for themselves and, in this way, do not allow us to feel what we're feeling. This is a projection of *their* desires.

Bitter realism is taking the pain and experiences that exist in the world and spreading a layer of toxic bitterness over everything.

Naive Idealism is wishing the world was a better place by covering reality in equally toxic sweetness.

Here again is the eternal yin and yang, good and evil, right and wrong, which is manifest in our world.

The eternal yin and yang will not change on this planet, no matter the extreme swings in desire from either end of the spectrum.

Staying centred in a world of extremes is extremely trying. It's the extremes that push our buttons - either the naively idealistic or the bitter realists.

THE ETERNAL BATTLE OF THE SEXES

8th December 2017

The battle of the sexes is so rampant in our world that we do not even realise it is there. It has become so endemic that we have become immune to its existence and we take it as the norm.

Snide remarks about the other gender, the things they do wrong, why they are only focused on one thing, and why the one takes advantage of the other. We are so quick to participate in the gender war that we have become immune to it — we have become unconscious about it.

It glares at us through our advertising, our movies, our theatre and, most importantly, it comes out of our mouths every day.

Every day, we make each other wrong. Every day, we raise our sons to a different standard from those we teach our daughters. Every day, we speak to women differently from the way we speak to men. We are so much a part of this gender war that we do not even know that we are co-creating it. I see the odd mom complaining about the clothes she can buy for her daughter and the occasional dad complaining about the toys they can choose from, or the books they can read.

I spent the last few months listening to and looking at our advertising, and I imagined that I could replace all the men in the ads with women and all the women with men, and I found that some of the advertising was simply ridiculous. We are stereotyping so badly that we do not even recognise it any longer.

I am saying that we are equal — not the same — equal. Unless we begin celebrating our differences and honouring them, and unless we stop making each other wrong, the world will continue to be a miserable place.

It is simply heart-breaking that we don't even know how to treat each other because over the last two thousand years we have done nothing but be disrespectful to each other. There are, of course, exceptions, but we live in a world that separates and divides us. I would love a world where we can be respectful of each other and let the differences shine through our equality.

FIND THAT ONE EFFORTLESS THING

16th December 2017

"If I did not sing, I'd never be able to clean out the dark places in my heart." Krishna Das.

If you do not know who he is, Google him. You won't regret it. What he says though, is that if we do that one thing that is effortless for us, then we are doing the thing that resonates with our whole self, or our soul.

Find that thing. We all have a thing. It does not have to be a majestic thing, it just has to be *that* thing. That thing: the thing we wake up for in the morning.

What do I mean by effortless? For sure, everything is effort. I do many things every day. Some things that I do, I like doing, such as sewing or cooking. Yet, even though I enjoy those things, they are not effortless. I like doing them and actually make time for them. I don't do them every day because I don't like doing them enough.

Other things I do take a huge amount of effort. I do them because I am a human being and I *have* to do them. For instance, washing dishes. Huge effort. Huge. I feel as if my arms are dragging on the floor as I walk to the basin. My heart is heavy, and I would much rather do something else, anything else. Huge Effort.

Then there is writing. For me, it is effortless. That doesn't mean that it does not consume energy, it does. But it also energises. It is pure effortlessness for me. Or teaching, which is effortless as well. Effortless. I do not write or teach because anybody else needs to read or learn something. I teach and write because it is that thing for me. As Krishna Das says, "It cleans out the dark places of my heart."

I'm so grateful that I know what my thing is.

WHAT I LEARNED THIS YEAR

24th December 2017

Tell people you love them; you never know when it's going to be their last day.

Try the other wine.

Veer away from your norm.

Take the risk and do that thing you've dreamed about but have not had the courage to do.

Let people love you back. It's all good and well to give — receiving is allowing others to show their love to you.

Everyone, and I mean everyone, goes through tough times. Be there for others.

I know this is a cliché, but seriously, don't sweat the small stuff.

I read that a house that is too clean is a health risk. The body needs a few germs to function optimally. No, seriously! Google it.

Eat fruit. I rediscovered this joy.

My body has changed. I'm learning to love it the way it is. I'm not 30 anymore, even though my head thinks I am.

Staying in pyjamas all day is not always a bad thing.

Ask for what you need to feel loved and respected. Very few of us are mind readers.

You can't *fight* to change things. You can only change things with love.

Say no to the things you do not want to do.

If you're going to do something, do it with your heart. If there is any resentment while doing it, you are doing it for the wrong reasons. Rather leave it.

Allow your body to heal at its own pace. If you are sick or have had surgery, let it be healed in its time. Your body knows what it needs. Pay attention.

Make the effort to spend time with family and friends. Yes, even the ones who never call you back. They need it the most.

Stop keeping score. If you keep a scorecard when doing something for others, you are not doing things out of love. You are negotiating a contract.

Time truly does make things more bearable. It does not heal all the wounds. It teaches you how to live around the loss.

Red lipstick changes everything.

Throw out your high heels.

Stop buying stuff. It clutters up your life. We all have too much stuff.

If you say you will do something, do it.

Be kind. Just be kind.

LEARN TO MANAGE YOUR CHEMISTRY

31st December 2017

Our bodies are hard-wired for flight or fight/freeze or fold. This is a fact. This is our biology. No matter how much we try to deny that, we simply can't. Our internal chemistry governs us. Fact. Our spiritual path cannot ever exclude the fact that we are in bodies that are hard-wired with chemistry.

If you focus your spirituality on your top three chakras only, you are wasting your time. Your heart chakra is the centre of your being. If you consistently only work on your top three chakras and you believe you will gain *enlightenment*, you are deluding yourself. Your heart chakra is the very centre of your existence on this planet. Your top three chakras and your bottom three chakras must all be in balance for you to have any real, meaningful experience on this planet. Being out of your body half the time does not serve you. And many *spiritual* people are half out of their bodies.

Our bodies continually release stress chemicals and hormones. The most consistent of these is cortisol. I believe it takes up to 12 hours for cortisol to dissipate out of our bodies. Unless and until we learn how to manage our body chemistry, none of the other spiritual practises, or mantra chanting, or positivity, will make an iota of difference.

Learn to get your body in balance first. Nothing else can occur unless and until your body is in a calm and peaceful state. It does not matter if you are trying to meditate and if you are chanting a mantra. If your body is in a state of distress, nothing you do will be effective.

Calm the body. Get your heart rate under control. Get the body into a state of balance – all the chakras – not just the top three. Once we get our body's chemistry under control, we can do the work... the work of healing, the work of love, the work of peace, and the work of growth.

You are in a physical body. It is pointless to try and do any of the work if your body is not in alignment with your soul. You are on this earth plane journey, and that means you need to learn how to manage being *in* your body. This is why you have a body. Learn how to make it calm and at ease. You can achieve nothing unless and until it is at ease.

CONCLUSION

Thank you for walking this path with me. It has been interesting for me going through this diary again and seeing what has changed in my life since I started the process of compiling this book. I took some bits out and left other bits in. The bits I took out were very personal and not relevant to this tome. I left the repeats in with the thought that if I repeated a theme, it was probably because I needed to hear the words again.

I think many writers write to formulate ideas and to bring them into their own awareness, and this is what this diary is about for me. It is to learn how my ideas about things change and how I can apply new knowledge in my life to my journey on planet earth more bearable.

It's hard to live here, on this planet. It's hard because of the rollercoaster ride of our emotions. The highs and the lows of loving and losing, the work of making a living, and trying to remain peaceful when we are exposed to so much distress.

It becomes a little easier if we know that we are not alone. If we know that we have the support of friends and family, without that, life would be empty and meaningless.

CONCLUSION

It is the love that we experience that makes this earthly journey worthwhile.

May you find love. Everyday.

ABOUT HILDA DE LA ROSA

Since 1992, Hilda de la Rosa has been a pioneer in the alternative health and wellbeing industry in South Africa. She started a healing centre in 1996 after her son was in a serious motor car accident. His near-death facilitated a huge shift in consciousness for Hilda and made her re-examine what's truly important in her life.

Hilda is known for her no-nonsense approach to spirituality and life and she often says, "If it does not make life better, why bother doing it?"

Hilda initially published her first book, Love Versus Fear in the USA in 2015. She decided to start her own publishing house, LK Publishers, in 2018 and its first title was the republication of Love Versus Fear. Not only is she publishing her own books but Hilda will help many authors get their work published in a slick and polished way.

Hilda's funny, quick witted, hard-hitting take on life, the Universe and everything will make you cry and it will make you laugh, but more importantly, it will make you think about, and examine your life.

ALSO BY HILDA DE LA ROSA

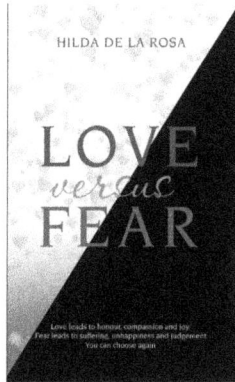

Jacqui Webb Says:

"What a roller coaster ride my journey with Love Versus Fear by Hilda de la Rosa has been. It leaves me in awe of the resilience of the human spirit and reminds me that s*** happens no matter how consciously, lovingly or creatively we live and love. This book can be seen as a manual for deeper insight into the nature of consciousness and provides a 'how to' model for conscious relating, which will serve to revolutionise and bless many relationships.

For me though, this book was an intense ride alongside the author as she sought to live in alignment with her highest inner voice. To love better, to learn always and to wring blessings for herself and humanity from every gut-wrenching, heart expanding moment of her journey.

It's elegantly written without self-pity, or over dramatisation. It's sharp, witty, intelligent and warm. Most of all, it is generous – generous to the other people who have been part of her story and generous to all of us, as it gifts us with the deep wisdom of a life well lived."

Coming in the third quarter of 2019: "Get Your Sh*t Together.